IAN AULD was unsurpassable on a football park in his youth. In 1958 he played in a Scottish Juvenile Select against England. He is the brother of Lisbon Lion Bertie Auld. Ian could have gone to Arsenal when he was 16, but went to the Balmore Bar at Saracen Cross instead. He played outside right and learned to write inside. After taking a wrong turn as a young man, Ian went on to rebuild his life. He married Eileen, and had two daughters, Sharon and Annette, and a son, Ian. An adoring husband and father, Ian was also a creative force, an actor and songwriter who wrote poems, short stories and sketches for a number of years before he passed away on 4 November 1998. Ian was a great fan of Joe Orton, as well as his beloved Celtic. *The Lions of Lisbon* was his only full-length play. His memory lives on in the stories he told and the family he loved.

WILLY MALEY is Professor of English Literature at the University of Glasgow. A critic, editor, teacher and writer, he was co-founder with the late Philip Hobsbaum of the Creative Writing Masters in 1995. *The Lions of Lisbon* is one of seven plays Willy has written collaboratively. Others include *From The Calton to Catalonia* (1990), which he wrote with his brother John Maley, based on their father's experiences as a POW during the Spanish Civil War, and *No Mean Fighter* (1992), a Scotsman Fringe First Winner at the Edinburgh Festival. A season ticket holder in the Lisbon Lions Stand, Willy was a columnist for the *Celtic View* during seasons 2003–2005. He contributed a hat-trick of essays to *Celtic Minded* volumes 1–3, and his poem 'Perfect Passing', a tribute to the late great Tommy Burns, was published in *The Celtic Opus* (2010). His most recent publication, also with Luath Press, is *Scotland and the Easter Rising*, co-edited with Kirsty Lusk.

The Lions of Lisbon *is suffused with a genuine interplay of* humour and pathos without becoming sentimental.
SIMON BERRY, *The Scotsman*

Far and away the greatest success
KEITH BRUCE

G000155355

The Lions of Lisbon

A Play of Two Halves

IAN AULD and WILLY MALEY

Luath Press Limited
EDINBURGH
www.luath.co.uk

First published 2017

ISBN: 978-1-910745-92-2

The paper used in this book is recyclable. It is made from
low chlorine pulps produced in a low energy, low emissions manner
from renewable forests.

Printed and bound by
Martins the Printers, Berwick-upon-Tweed

Typeset in 10 point Frutiger by
3btype.com

This book is dedicated to

Ian Auld (1942–1998).

Still playing on the wing.

Contents

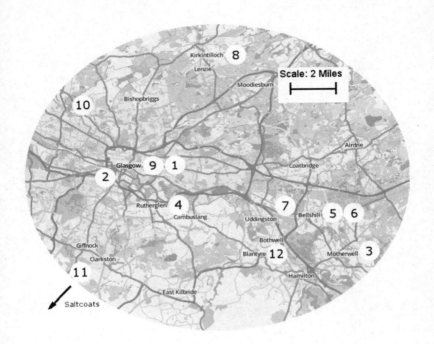

The Lions of Lisbon – Local Heroes

1 Ronald 'Ronnie' Campbell Simpson (Goalkeeper) KING'S PARK

2 James 'Jim' Philip Craig (Right Back) GOVAN

3 Thomas 'Tommy' Gemmell (Left back) MOTHERWELL

4 Bobby Murdoch (Midfielder) RUTHERGLEN

5 William 'Billy' McNeill (Celtic Captain and Defender) BELLSHILL

6 John Clark (Left half) BELLSHILL

7 James Connolly 'Jimmy' Johnstone (Outside right) VIEWPARK

8 William Semple Brown 'Willie' Wallace (Inside forward) KIRKINTILLOCH

9 Thomas Stephen 'Stevie' Chalmers (Centre forward) GARNGAD

10 Robert 'Bertie' Auld (Outside left/Midfielder) MARYHILL

11 Robert 'Bobby' Lennox (Outside left) SALTCOATS

12 John Fallon (Substitute Goalkeeper, not used) BLANTYRE

All of the Lisbon Lions grew up within 30 miles of Parkhead.

The Lions of Lisbon is a play of two halves telling the story of Celtic's famous 1967 European Cup victory over Inter Milan. The significance of the match cannot be denied. How did the lucky ones who were there to see history being made make their way to Lisbon? From selling spearmint chewing gum and macaroon bars to pawning the chapel's candlesticks, the importance of football is reflected in the fans' determination to get to the greatest game of all and the lasting effect it has on their lives.

The play opens and closes with Danny and his son Sean on their way to Celtic Park in 1992, on the occasion of the silver anniversary of Lisbon, with the action in between established as one long flashback. The play is about laughter and about love, just as much for the beautiful game of football as for the people who make it worthwhile and, on occasion, make it very special.

This play commemorates a game of football that makes memories, makes history, and – for those who meet their match in more ways than one – makes life.

Production History

The Lions of Lisbon was first staged by The Penny Mob
Theatre Company, on tour, 23 April–14 June 1992,
including a week at The Arches Theatre at Mayfest and a
week at the Tron Theatre, 9–14 June; subsequently at the
Pavilion Theatre, Glasgow, 15–26 September 1992. It
played to a total audience of 10,000. Directed by Libby
McArthur. Reviewed in *The Herald*, *The Scotsman*, *The
Guardian*, *The Evening Times*; revived by Basement
Theatre Company (Renfrew), directed by Heather
Morrison, with performances at the Fitzgerald Centre,
Greenock, 16 March, Cottiers Theatre, Glasgow, 22–24
March, and Paisley Arts Centre, Paisley, 29–31 March
2012; and again by No Nonsense Productions, directed by
Kevin Jannetts, Greenock Celtic Supporters Club, 30
September 2016.

Introduction

In the autumn of 1991, I got talking to Ian Auld, Bertie's brother, who had himself been a talented footballer in his youth. Ian had written some poems and short stories, and was keen to try his hand at something on a grander scale. He'd also done some acting and had a feel for what worked onstage. With the silver anniversary of Celtic's sensational European Cup Victory looming, Ian and I talked about ways of celebrating that amazing occasion. We'd both caught *The Celtic Story* at the Pavilion during the centenary year, and we decided to try to capture on stage some of the energy and excitement of Lisbon, and see if we could bring to life some of the stories we'd heard over the years. Ian was a bit older than me so we had two different streams of patter running together, which was great for capturing the mood of the time. That's how *The Lions of Lisbon* got started, from our conversations over the course of several months between the autumn of 1991 and the spring of 1992. We were drawing on memory, in my case childhood memory, the memory of one of the many stay-at-home fans in 1967. In Ian's case the memory of someone who was there, and the brother of one of the Celtic players who would become legends after Lisbon. Our dialogues, at the end of which we were often breathless with laughter, were the basis of the scenes we drafted in those first few months of our friendship.

The strange thing about theatre is the way it brings voices back to life. Ian passed away in 1998, but reading through the script again, and then hearing the lines spoken aloud, I was back once more with him in his house in Milton and in the local library and the

Unemployed Workers' Centre in 1992, hammering out the lines that made us laugh till we cried. We were at different ages and stages of life but we hailed from the same part of Glasgow and had the same passion for Celtic.

When we sat down to write the play 25 years ago Lisbon seemed further away than it does now. It felt like history. Now, with the Jock Stein and Lisbon Lions stands at Celtic Park, the statue of Billy McNeill on the Celtic Way, and the 'Sixty-seven' song belted out on the terraces, there's a real sense of living memory and of history being played out in the present. When the play was staged in 1992 the whole team turned up at the Tron Theatre to see it. That was an unforgettable moment. In Ian's words, 'it was the icing on the cake'.

The play is doubly 'dated' when you think about it. Written in 1992 and set between 1992 and 1967, the action of the play is one long flashback to events in Lisbon. And now, 25 years on, it feels like one of those Monty Python sketches where you get a flashback within a flashback. The framing device of 1992 has become, itself, historical. Any new production of a play has to take into account the passage of the intervening years but this is especially true of one that is tied to a particular event. Just as the play in 1992 made much of the gap between the '60s and the '90s, so the play of today must remind us of the gap between the '90s and now. The fact that some of the 'in-jokes' of '92 are out of date – like the macaroon bars the wide-boys try to sell in Lisbon – just adds another layer to the cake.

Now that *The Lions of Lisbon* is finally being published as a book 25 years after it was first staged, there's an additional section entitled '67 on '67' which features a range of voices reflecting on Celtic's unique achievement. Fans from a variety of backgrounds and occupations were asked to say in 67 words what '67 meant to them. I think their statements capture beautifully the way Lisbon has resonated down the years for families, communities and individuals. Ian's widow, Eileen Auld, contributed 67 words and more. Her support for the play and the publication has been as invaluable as it was back in the day when she supplied Ian and me with half-time refreshments.

The Lions of Lisbon is a play with a happy ending. It's a celebration and a big-hearted belly laugh and, as I've said, writing it with Ian was great fun. Although the history and memories are inevitably tinged with sadness at the fact that he and some of the others involved are no longer with us, I'm really glad the play is being revived after twenty-five years. We made something that's lasted. And Ian, if you're watching under the floodlights, you know you'll never walk alone.

Willy Maley
January 2017

Acknowledgements

Every book takes teamwork and this one is down to some terrific supporters cheering it on every step of the way. First and foremost a huge thank you is due to Eileen Auld and Dini Power for their encouragement in getting the play back on the road again. Thanks to Paul Cuddihy, Paul English, Jim Lister, Martin McCardie, Gavin MacDougall and Stephen Wright for playing their part. Hats off to those who were able to say in 67 words exactly what '67 means to them. Special thanks to Hilary Bell and Jennie Renton at Luath who helped get the book over the goal line with great aplomb. Finally, all hail the Lisbon Lions for the amazing achievement that inspired this play, and the fans who make the club's history so special. Let's make some noise for the Bhoys!

The Line-Up

Cathy Boyle

Celtic supporter from the Gorbals, wants to be a nun, but comes back from Lisbon the wiser

Donaldo Gaberdini

Inter Milan fan and ice-cream vendor from Largs

Keith Chinwag

English sports commentator who thinks Celtic are the Best of British

Phil Divers

Celtic supporter from Possilpark, as wide as the Clyde

Terry Docherty

Celtic supporter from the Garngad, a devout chancer

Fiona Farquhar

Secretary of Larkhall Conservative Association, a blue-rinsed battleaxe

Hector Farquhar

Her husband, a police Inspector, bitter Orangeman, and Rangers diehard

Danny Gallagher

Celtic supporter from Donegal, a mammy's boy

Sean Gallagher

Danny's son, made in Lisbon

Theresa Kelly

Celtic supporter from the Gallowgate, young and upwardly nubile

Father O'Hara

Celtic supporter and Gorbals priest, a self-confessed football hooligan

Chorus   In May 1967, 10,000 of the greatest supporters in the world embarked on the most important crusade since the quest for the Holy Grail. They hailed from Scotland, Ireland and every corner of the globe. Most were Celtic daft. Some were just plain daft. All of them would have followed the Magnificent Eleven to the ends of the earth. Two thousand miles was a dawdle.

The Celticade stretched from the Campsie Fells to the Pyrenees. The support unrolled like a green carpet across England, France and Spain. Those who couldn't afford to go by plane flew by the arse of their trousers. They travelled on slow boats and long-distance lorries, in battered vans and buses, in used cars and trains that never ran on time, on rusty bikes and blistered feet. Whole streets were lifted from Glasgow's East End and transported across land and sea, from one dear green place to another.

The fans lived on borrowed time and money, on a pilgrimage that would take them to the Pearly Gates and back again. They arrived in Lisbon with a fistful of escudos and a heartful of hope. As far as they were concerned, they had not left their families or communities behind. They were married to Celtic and pregnant with passion. The club was their kith and kin, their neighbour, their best friend, their ticket to immortality. They came clutching floodlit memories. They came over broken glass and stones, walking on water and living on a prayer. They came in search of paradise and found it in Portugal.

1

Danny's Boy

[Danny Gallagher, an Irishman in his forties, and his son, Sean, a Glaswegian in his mid-twenties, are on their way to Parkhead]

Danny
You've made us miss the bus again. You're a helluva slowcoach, son. You don't know if yer hummin or hawin. You'd be late for your own funeral.

Sean
We'll get there alright. Keep yer teeth in. If ye helped me buy a motor we'd have no worries gettin there.

Danny
You get a job and you can buy a motor.

Sean
Ah cannae get a motor off a grant. It was you and ma maw that wanted me tae go tae Yooni.

Danny
That's right. We wanted ye to better yerself. A motor'll come in good time.

	Meanwhile, what's wrong with a transcard?
Sean	Here we go.
Danny	If public transport is good enough for yer old da, it's good enough for you.
Sean	This is 1992. They've taken the trams off, ye know. Aw ma pals have got motors.
Danny	Some bloody pals they are. Won't even give a fella a lift.
Sean	They're no taxi drivers, Dad … Hey, did you read that thing in the paper about the Lisbon Lions? They're looking for people's memories.
Danny	Are they now? Don't look at me. I lost mine years ago.
Sean	Come on, da. You must have more stories than the Red Road flats. Lisbon. That's where you and ma maw met. You must have a few crackers to tell.
Danny	Crackers, is it? Ah suppose I have. It's a long time past, though, boy. Things is changed. It's a different ball game now – big business, so it is. If someone had told me I'd be paying six quid to stand at a football match twenty-five years ago I'd have thought they were crazy. A working man can hardly afford to follow football now. No wonder the crowds have gone down.

Sean	Ach, yer two-faced, da. How come yer still goin?
Danny	Because I've nothing better to do.
Sean	Tell me about it.
Danny	Because it keeps me out yer mother's hair.
Sean	Heard it.
Danny	Because where would a poor man be without his wee taste of paradise on a Saturday afternoon?
Sean	Nowhere.
Danny	I'll tell you this much, though. It's not a punter's paradise any more. Them bloody yuppies have taken over. The style of play has changed as well. Where are the attacking full backs, the out-and-out strikers, the dribbling wingers? No team in Scotland could lift the European Cup now, I'll tell you that much. Not Rangers, with their big money and their big stadium. And Celtic have enough trouble getting into Europe these days, never mind winning anything.
Sean	But what about the Lisbon Lions, da? That was some team.
Danny	Sure it was a grand old team.
Sean	The greatest team on earth.
Danny	The greatest club on earth.
Sean	A team of individuals.
Danny	But Celtic's bigger than any wan

individual, Sean. Bigger than any team. It's a club with a great tradition. The Lisbon Lions didn't come out of the blue, or the green for that matter. It was eighty years of history that lifted that cup in Lisbon. Celtic history. The Club. From its founders to its fans. Brother Walfrid, Willie Maley, and all the others. Names that'll live on beyond any single defeat or victory.

Sean	But Lisbon was special, da. Ye must admit. The first British Club tae win the European Cup. And you were there. Was that no something else?
Danny	Aye, it was something else alright. But it's no use harping on about the past. It's not fair to the lads that have to look after Celtic's future. They'll make their own history. Europe will ring tae the name of Celtic again.
Sean	But da, you're lucky to have Lisbon to look back on. A taste of paradise. A man could die happy after that. Ah wish ah'd been there. Ah must've seen the video a thousand times. And to think that you were there, da. It must a been a religious experience.
Danny	You could say that. We were crucified wae the heat, ah mind that.
Sean	Was ma maw next tae you oan the terracin? How did yez meet? Whit a day that must hiv been.

Danny	Aye, it was a day and a half right enough... Come on, we'd be as quick walking.
Sean	Tell me about Lisbon, da –
Danny	I'll save me breath. We're late for the match.
Sean	Sure, ye can walk and talk at the same time, which is more than Ian Ferguson can do.
Danny	Okay, Sean. But if we miss a goal you're a stretcher case.

[Exit]

'I was an immigrant. I was twenty-one, but in my mind, I was a Bluesman, playing in Canadian cafés, too cool to care about football – until Celtic won the European Cup. It was almost unbelievable – eleven Scotsmen beat a bunch of multi-national millionaires! Twenty years later, Jack McGinn would be in the Wildcat office, asking if we'd be interested in writing The Celtic Story. Rest? History...'

DAVE ANDERSON
ACTOR, PLAYWRIGHT, JAZZ MUSICIAN

'I was six years old when the final whistle blew on a 2–1 victory. The Lisbon Lions, a team of twelve true Scotsmen, made world history! I went on to marry the brother of Bertie Auld in 1984. A true and talented husband and father with a passion for Celtic like no other. His legacy, together with the Celtic story and the spirit of Lisbon, lives on.'

EILEEN AULD
FAN

' It was the year football became sexy.
The Lions were an explosion of a team
– revolutionaries daring to recast the game
in glorious tribute to the tanner ba' players of
old. They may have kicked off in black and white
but Jock Stein's men shone in bright technicolor
under the Portuguese sun. All was changed
– Celtic were now a club of all Scotland
and all the world. '

DOUGLAS BEATTIE
JOURNALIST

' Hendrix. Sergeant Pepper. Pink Floyd. Summer of
Love. Scotland beating England, then world
champions, at Wembley. Baxter playing keepie-
uppie. The Lisbon Lions, who, to someone
growing up as a Rangers supporter, were the
phantom presence in every conversation with
Celtic fans. Bigger than Nine-in-a-Row. Bigger
than Rangers' Cup Winners' Cup side of 1972.
An unrepeatable feat. A golden stick with which
to beat us. An immortal irritation. '

ALAN BISSETT
WRITER

‘ British colonialism in Ireland, Great Irish Hunger, immigration to Scotland, refugees, starvation, poverty, discrimination, prejudice, bigotry and racism. Celtic! A risen people. Green and white. The shamrock, the Irish tricolour. Family, community, songs of love, rebellion, joy, happiness and celebration. History, heritage, memory, pride, respect and esteem. Europe, Lisbon '67, champions! Glory: victory on the field of dreams. Always the same, forever changed, utterly. Thank you God. ,

JOSEPH M. BRADLEY
ACADEMIC

‘ Eleven local boys who overcame defensive drabness to conquer Europe with unstoppable attacking play that was a victory for football everywhere. Bertie Auld starting 'The Celtic Song' in the tunnel. While the Scottish establishment treated the Irish as second class citizens, the Lions defeated this with beautiful, uplifting football that gave us back our pride. Part of the fairy tale that makes Celtic a life-long love affair. ,

STEPHEN BREEN
MANAGING DIRECTOR

2

Hector's House

[*Hector and Fiona Farquhar. Half-plain, half-pan*]

Fiona   There's a letter for you, Hector. It's oan
         the mantelpiece.

Hector   I told you no to leave my correspondence
         oan the mantelpiece, Fiona. It could fall
         into the fire and burn with disastrous
         consequences. Important documents
         could be loast. Demotion could follow.

Fiona   But Hector, I always use an ornament as
         a paperweight. Your letter's under the
         lucky horseshoe that Catriona gied us as
         a wedding present.

Hector   It wouldn't be a lucky horseshoe if my
         mail ended up in ashes, Fiona. Now, let's

29

	see what we've goat here. (*He opens the letter*) It's from the Chief Constable.
Fiona	Oh Hector. It'll be about Nuremberg. We'll be able to visit Alasdair's regiment. It's so wonderful. A working holiday. It's absolutely magic. A dream come true.
Hector	Hold it, Fiona. There must be some mistake.
Fiona	What is it, Hector? You've gone a funny colour.
Hector	'Dear Inspector Farquhar, Further to your request to attend the European Cup Winners' Cup Final in Nuremberg, I regret to inform you that, after consultation with the Assistant Chief Constable I have decided to refuse permission on this occasion...'
Fiona	... Oh Hector, it's no fair! You really wanted to see the Teddy Bears lift that trophy!
Hector	(*Holding up a restraining hand*)... Quiet, woman – there's more. 'I feel that your expertise would be better employed at the European Cup Final in Lisbon. I am sure you will agree that the policing of this event could command your undivided attention in a way that the match in West Germany would not.'
Fiona	Oh Hector!
Hector	Oh Fiona!

Fiona	Oh fuck!... What'll they say at the station?
Hector	What'll they say at the Lodge?

[Lights out]

" When I was at secondary school Celtic won the
European Cup every May. They showed it each
year in the assembly hall at the Greg off an old
school cine-projector. We gave it our complete
and unbridled attention. It was the only time
they ever got us to shut up, the only thing I ever
really learned from school that has stayed with
me till this day. "

EDDIE BURNS
TEACHER

" Lisbon is memorable to me only because I wasn't
there. Billy McNeill arranged my ticket but the
BBC wouldn't allow me to leave the country.
(I was then playing *This Man Craig* in Glasgow.)
So, on the night, I watched on my bedroom
TV with a bottle of wine and orders not to be
interrupted. I remember yet every thrilling
moment – especially when Jim 'Cairney'
Craig scored! "

JOHN CAIRNEY
ACTOR

" Chan fhaca mi an geam',oir cha robh telebhisean againn, agus bha mi robh òg son a dhol dhan taigh-seinnse, *An Lobster Pot* 'san Òban, far am faca mo bhràthair bu shine e. Ach thuig mi gun robh e 'na dhearbhadh air an rud ionadail: gum faodadh òganaich bhon an tuath a bhith mar Stevie Chalmers agus an gnothach a dheanamh air Catenaccio fuar Gallda sam bith. "

AONGHAS PHÀDRAIG CAIMBEUL
WRITER

" I didn't see the match because we didn't have a telly, and I was too young to go to the pub (*The Lobster Pot* in Oban) where my older brother watched it. But I understood it was a triumph of the local, and that a peasant boy from the islands could defeat any alien Catenaccio system by running forward with the ball until a goal was scored. "

ANGUS PETER CAMPBELL
WRITER

3

Confessions of a Justified Sinner

[*Father O'Hara, in a state of undress, braces dangling, ironing his cassock, singing snatches of 'Bachelor Boy'*]

Father O'Hara   (*Testing the iron with his finger and burning it*) Ma heid's like a toayshoap. Ah'm tellin ye. Ah don't know if it's New York or New Year. Work. Work. Work. It's hard graft. It's no as if ah've goat the weekend aff. Sunday's a killer. Ah should get double time fur that. Time an a hauf fur a Seterday. Then there's the backshift. Nae bonus or nothin. Hauf the time ah'm doon oan ma hunkers. Werr an terr oan the joints. Ah've had tae gie up the five-a-sides.

[*There's a knocking offstage*]

Nae peace fur the wicked.

[*Father O'Hara puts on his cassock, revealing his occupation to the audience*]

[*Another knock*]

Ah hear ye... Ah don't know. Everybody wants tae go tae heaven, but naebody wants tae die.

[*Cathy Boyle goes into the box*]

Cathy Forgive me father, for I have sinned. It's a day since my last confession.

Father O'Hara That's no long.

Cathy It was a long day.

Father O'Hara Tell me aboot it. Ah've been up since six o'clock. You think you've got problems...

Cathy Father O'Hara. This is ma confession. You're supposed tae listen.

Father O'Hara Naebody wants tae know aboot ma problems.

Cathy Ah'm goin away, Faither, an ah'm no tellin ma faimly. Ah'm givin up ma joab an takin the wages fae ma week's lyin time. Ah've pawned ma maw's rings. Ah've stole two bikinis oot a Woolworths. Ah've sold aw ma brother's Beatles albums. And tae cap it aw, ah've split up wae ma fiancé because he kicked wae the wrang fit.

Father O'Hara Ah take it yer fiancé was a footballer?

Cathy Naw. He was a Protestant.

Father O'Hara Ah see. He widnae be a footballer then.

Cathy We got engaged at Christmas. We were to be married in September.

Father O'Hara Mixed marriages are often fraught wae difficulty.

Cathy	This wan was gonnae be dead fraught.
Father O'Hara	The minute a man an woman get thegither ye can expect trouble. You've done the right thing, my dear. The single life makes sense these days. I don't know how young couples can make ends meet.
Cathy	It's Lisbon ah'm goin tae, Faither.
Father O'Hara	Lisbon! Hiv ye goat a ticket for the match?
Cathy	Its a package deal. Aw inclusive. Fifty-seven quid.
Father O'Hara	Fifty-seven quid! That's a bit steep.
Cathy	Its been an uphill struggle gettin the cash thegither.
Father O'Hara	That's a sin. Ah mean, that's a shame. I gather that Theresa Kelly is going to share the spoils wae ye. I've a good mind tae take they bikinis off ye. Say Ten Hail Marys. And 20 Hail! Hails!
Cathy	Thanks Father.

[*She goes out*]

Father O'Hara	That lassie wid get ye intae trouble. Ah might wear ma shirt back tae front, but ma heid disnae button up the back. A week's lying time, eh? Ah don't even get a long lie oan a Sunday. Wid ye believe a wiz the smartest boay at school? Look at the nick ae me noo, wearin a dufflecoat tied wae a bit a claes rope. Ah've nothing tae gie up for Lent but the ghost. There's

nae perks in ma joab, unless ye want a candle-lit dinner. The candles are nae problem, but the dinner's no so easy to come by. Ah've nae other mouths tae feed, right enough. Ah don't need tae worry aboot a family. Ah'll hiv nobody tae look efter me in ma auld age. Ma da always wanted me tae be a white collar worker. Ah think he had a desk-joab wae the toon cooncil in mind. But ah had other ideas. Ah used tae look up at the priest at mass an think, 'Ah want tae be up there'. You shoulda seen ma mother's face when ah came in fae school an told her ah wiz gonnae be a Faither. [*Pause*]

God, ah'm tired. Ah've had three funerals, two baptisms, four communions, and umpteen confessions. Ah'm dyin oan ma feet. (*Looks up at the ceiling*) Ah could crucify they bandits that took the lead aff the roof. That's aw ah need. A spyhole fur the eye in the sky. The Big Yin disnae miss a trick as it is. Noo he can see right in. (*Shrugs, raising his hands, palms upwards*) Look, we've been through aw this before. Glasgow Celtic are a good Catholic club, founded by a priest as a charitable organisation. Ah'm duty-bound tae go. Football is of great spiritual comfort to this community, and I'm sure my flock won't mind contributing to my passage seeing it's for a good cause. I told them the score oan Sunday. (*Steps forward and blesses himself*) Thanks tae

Celtic, the takings at Mass have doubled in the last week, wae silver collections every day. It's gettin so ah can hardly lift the plate. Ah don't know where people get the money fae. Actually, ah dae know. They confess. Anyhow, it seems only fair that it should go towards giving them support. And it's only right that the Church should have a man in Lisbon, especially when so many of the faith are going. I'll be keeping an eye on a few of my own parishioners. I'm gonnae visit the shrine of Fatima. Two birds wae wan stone, if ye get ma meaning. It would be daft fur me tae stay at home while so many young, vulnerable people were travelling so many miles. I have to be there to lend a guiding hand. A laudable sacrifice, I'm sure ye'll agree. (*Steps back again*) This dog collar isnae welded oan. (*Loosening his collar and removing his cassock*). Ah'm gonnae let maself aff the leash in Lisbon. Ah'd like tae be Cesar fur a day. (*Heading an imaginary ball*) Soarin like an eagle. King of the air. That much closer tae Heaven. Watchin the Celtic go forward. Ah'll tell ye wan thing, there'll be a revolving door oan this chapel come Thursday mornin. It'll be the fastest mass in living memory. If ah miss ma flight there'll no be a swear-box big enough tae take the sharp end ae ma tongue.

[Lights out]

'
Sixty Seven
Was football heaven
For the best eleven
In green and white.
I wasn't here
That special year
But the aul dear
Recounts the sight.
The faith, the fears,
The songs, the beers,
The Celtic cheers
Rang out all night,
The legacy
Of Tommy G
And Stevie C
Remains alright.
I never fail
To love that tale
Now the cry 'Hail Hail'
Has become my right. '

ROISÌN COLL
ACADEMIC

'I never went. Our youngest was four months, our first two and a half. After Inter's penalty there was a toot outside. My wife's driving lesson. Springburn was silent. When she got back we'd triumphed. Up to the Mungo Club – place was rocking. BBC highlights on a 15-inch screen. I don't know who started the song: 'We've got the best team in the land'. What a night!'

HARRY CONNOLLY
BUCHANAN BRIDGE CLUB

'Irish? No. Catholic? No. Football-supporting parents? No. But for the European Cup win, I probably wouldn't support Celtic. My English father was thrilled by Jock Stein's transformation of a directionless squad into one that claimed the biggest prize of all in two years. His account sowed the seeds of a lifelong passion in an impressionable five year old. Occasionally I curse him. Most of the time, I'm pretty grateful.'

DONALD COWEY
JOURNALIST

"I cried when Stevie Chalmers scored the winning goal. The house erupted as the ball hit the net and I started bawling. I was ten months old. I wasn't alone, though; my parents, my gran, aunts and uncles, generations whose support of Celtic was part of their identity, all shedding tears as we became the Kings of Europe. It still makes me cry now, when I think of it."

PAUL CUDDIHY
EDITOR *CELTIC VIEW*

"My grandfather Tommy Reilly was a scout for Celtic late '60s early '70s and a friend of Jock Stein. I remember as a kid he brought out a pair of white Umbro shorts with a green 5 on front and back, Billy McNeill's of course. Watching black and white replays of Lisbon still brings a tear to my eye, knowing that my Papa was there that day."

TONY CURRAN
ACTOR

4

A Blue Do

[*Hector is on the phone to the Chief Constable*]

Hector
But Sir. Surely there's been some mistake. I'm a master mark freemason. I've been on the square. Lodge number 1–690. I've had my knuckles crushed by the Duke of Kent. You've shaken me by the elbow on a number of occasions… You know how old my granny is. You've seen my wee bit of dirt… Yes. I see…

Your wife, Sir… Yes… It was very foolish of me, Sir… I had no idea who she was… I'll return the stockings at once, Sir. Yes… Destroy the negatives, yes. Consider it done… Bicycle clips, Sir. Yes. I'll look them out… No, not a word… Goodbye.

[*Fiona enters*]

Fiona	Any luck?
Hector	I'm afraid my luck has run out, Fiona. If I had a gun, I'd put myself out of my misery.
Fiona	Oh Hector! That would be a crying shame!
Hector	Me no going to Nuremberg is a crying shame. I think I'll go out and fit up a few mugs. [*He puts his truncheon and a few other weapons inside his jacket*] Once more onto the beat.
Fiona	Oh Hector. I hate to see you like this. It couldnae happen to a nicer man.
Hector	Can you picture it if they bead-rattlers win?
Fiona	I shudder to think. It would be absolutely unbearable.
Hector	They'll be singing 'Hail! Hail!' from Lisbon to John O'Groats.
Fiona	I didn't think there were any Catholics as far up as John O'Groats.
Hector	You know, Fiona. For a woman who knits such lovely balaclavas you can be helluva stupid. If O'Groats isn't an Irish name I'll eat my sash.
Fiona	What about Tam O'Shanter?
Hector	A drunken, superstitious Fenian.

Fiona   Watch your blood pressure, Hector.
             Remember what the doctor said. You've
             no to get upset.

Hector   No bloody wonder. What is the world
             coming to? They're talking about
             putting men on the moon, and they
             can't even keep Catholics out of the
             shipyards. This is my country, Fiona. Ah
             fought for it.

Fiona   I thought you worked in the Post Office?

Hector   I was doing ma bit, Fiona. I was doing it
             for Britain. [*He turns to go, and farts*] I
             told you about that gingerbread, Fiona.
             Can't you make it without nuts? It gives
             me heartburn.

             [He goes off. Lights out]

'67 is having one star above our crest meaning Celtic are better than all the rest. It's knowing Lisbon means more to you than anyone else and knowing it'll never be repeated without ridiculous wealth. Lisbon is a badge of honour worn with pride even if you weren't there for the ride. It means Simpson, Craig, McNeill, Clark, Gemmell, Murdoch, Auld, Johnstone, Wallace, Chalmers, Lennox and Stein.

MARTIN DALZIEL
REPORTER, *CELTIC VIEW*

Too young for the Summer of Love, and with about as much chance of going to Lisbon as San Francisco, in that analogue decade of New Towns and neighbours and the watchful solidarity of the 'two nights and a Sunday' overtime men, I moved between houses and fuzzy television sets spellbound as those words 'Glasgow' and 'Celtic' entered forever the dictionary of the age. I was there.

BOB DAVIS
ACADEMIC

> I was 22 and my main memory is of uninhibited joy at the final whistle among the family all glued to the TV. My other recollection was of the pride which many of our non-Celtic supporting neighbours took in the achievement, seeing it as a triumph for Scotland. 1967 was a key factor in the long story of the emancipation of the Catholic Irish in this country.

SIR TOM DEVINE
HISTORIAN

> Every time I see highlights of this match, I greet. Every time I think of the players in the tunnel singing the 'The Celtic Song' before going out, I greet. Every time I think of how they played that day and the goals scored, I greet. Every time I think of Billy McNeill, all alone, lifting the big cup, I greet. It's my happiest memory of football.

PHILIP DIFFER
WRITER

" Two weeks before my seventh birthday
something spread a Christmas tingle in May.
At that age it was all about feeling. Meaning
came later. A black and white coin
operated telly, crouched silence, held breath,
streets deserted. Cheers. Bit lips. Rosaries from
the women. A frightening cheer and tear
choked throats. The Coatbridge Irish filtered
onto streets blinking like a people emerging
from the dust of war. "

DES DILLON
WRITER

●

" 25 May 1967, aged nine, I realised I was rich.
My extended family and everyone from our close
and neighbouring closes watched the Lions on
our TV. Big screen, big room, kettle, and no
doubt big glasses. The moment we won, all the
kids, including the girls, ran down to replay the
match – our wee back court as big and mythic
as a stadium in far Portugal. "

CHRIS DOLAN
WRITER

5

El Posso

Possilpark

[*Phil and Terry are trying to find a way of getting to Lisbon, and asking themselves why*]

Phil   Ye know, Terry, when ah stoap tae think sometimes, ah say tae maself, 'Whit am ah daein gaun oot, knoackin ma pan in five days a week, when ma only pleasure is the Celtic?'

Terry   That's your trouble, Phil. You think too much. Ah'm a doer, no a thinker.

Phil   That's right. Yer aye gettin done.

Terry   If there's a way of gettin tae Lisbon ah'll find it, trust me.

Phil   Ah dae. As far as ah can throw ye.

Terry	Ah wish ye could shy a baw like big Yogi, an ye could throw me right acroass Europe, aw the way tae Lisbon.
Phil	Why dae we dae it, Terry? Why are we willin tae sacrifice everythin fur 90 minutes?
Terry	There's aw sorts a reasons, Phil. When things urnae goin right at work, ur at hame, can ye call yer boss a bastard, ur yer da?
Phil	Under yer breath, mibbe.
Terry	Mibbe. But at Parkheid oan a Seterday, ye can call the referee for everything withoot fear a comeback or contradiction. Because yer wan ae the bhoys.
Phil	There's strength in numbers. That's a fact.
Terry	Exactly. When yer staunin there wae 50,000 punters like yersell, ye know ye'll never walk alone.
Phil	That's right. Yer aw in the same boat. Up shit creek withoot a paddle.
Terry	Ye nail yer colours tae the mast, and get yer oar in.
Phil	Full steam ahead.
Terry	Win or lose, ye've only a week tae wait fur another bite at the cherry.
Phil	Wan minute yer doon, an the baw's up oan the slates.

Terry	Next minute yer up, an there's everything tae play fur.
Phil	It's great tae be oan the winnin side.
Terry	It's great tae be oan the wan side, Phil. Nae complications. Everything's black an white. Ur green an white. Then ye go hame. Yer maw an da are fighting. Ye don't know who tae support.
Phil	Yer right, Terry. It's nice tae know whose side yer oan, an who's oan yer side.
Terry	Course it is. Life's hard, is it no?
Phil	Yer no kiddin. Workin yer arse aff, day in, day oot, tryin tae make ends meet.
Terry	An the Celtic make things simple.
Phil	So they dae. If only getting tae Lisbon was simple.
Terry	Where there's a will there's a way.
Phil	Withoot money there's no way, José. If we can make money, we're minted.
Terry	Quoted.
Phil	But how can we claw in enough tae go tae Portugal in a couple a weeks? Time's runnin oot.
Terry	Ma da says ah can watch it oan the telly. Says ah'll get a better view ae the game than him. Says he'll bring me back a programme an the stub ae his ticket. Ah telt him where tae pit it.
Phil	The ticket?

Terry	Naw, the telly. He's always wanted the aerial power a Billy McNeill.
Phil	Yer yer da's double, Terry.
Terry	Are you tryin tae start a fight?
Phil	Naw, ah'm tryin tae get you tae the game at yer da's expense. If ah wiz you, ah'd tie him up in the coal-bunker an fly aff wae his passport.
Terry	It's easier said than done, Phil. He eats a lot mer than me. Ah jist get scraps, ye know. It saves him keepin a dug.
Phil	Ma da's no goin because ae his back. It's knackered wae cerryin your da hame fae the pub.
Terry	Mine's is knackered wae cerryin you in the pub.
Phil	Ah wish ye wid cerry me tae Lisbon. If ah need tae walk in ma bare feet acroass broken gless ah'll be at that game, Terry.
Terry	Can ah get yer shoes? They must be worth a pound in the pawn. It aw adds up.
Phil	There's goat tae be some way a gettin there that we hivnae thoat ae.
Terry	Whit aboot the bank?
Phil	Ah've no goat an account.
Terry	Can ye get yer hauns oan a pair a stockins?
Phil	Hiv you been readin ma diary?

Terry	Naw, bit ah've been thinkin a makin a big withdrawal doon at the Cross.
Phil	Ah'm no walkin alang Saracen Street wae a stoackin oan ma face. They'd aw know it wiz me.
Terry	Jist kid oan it's a tan. Don't try tae light up a fag, but.
Phil	It's too dodgy, Terry. Ye don't shite oan yer ain doorstep. Whit aboot the Garngad? There must be some ae your mates able tae help ye oot.
Terry	Are ye kiddin? They aw remembered that ah owed them money the minute Celtic qualified.
Phil	It's every fan fur themselves.
Terry	Ah asked fur money fur ma birthday. Ah thoat that might pull in a few greenbacks.
Phil	But yer birthday's no tae October.
Terry	Ah know. That was the snag.
Phil	Ma uncle had a win oan the hoarses, but by the time ah goat doon tae the Calton it wiz aw drunk. The bastard had the hard neck tae tap me fur a taxi.
Terry	Some guys take saftness fur daftness, Phil. Ye need tae wisen up. Ye've goat tae be oan the ball where money's concerned.
Phil	He made me think ae the bookies, though, ma uncle. Ah've goat a line oan

	Inter tae score first. If they don't ah'll no mind, but if they dae it's a wee earner. Softens the blow, dinnit?
Terry	Ye better no turn oot tae be a Jonah.
Phil	Don't worry. We'll hiv a whale ae a time. The Celts'll run them intae the grun.
Terry	An we'll be there tae see it. Ah'm no hingin aboot here wae a big green face. Ah'm Joe the Toff as soon as ah get ma fare thegither.
Phil	Ah'll rack ma brains the night, Terry. Ah'm every bit as keen as you tae get there. Ye know that. But ah don't fancy hivin Farquhar gien me the third degree through thirty denier.
Terry	Put it this way, whitever way we get there, we'll get away fae that big bastard ae a polis fur a foartnight. If we get tae Lisbon an he buggers aff tae Nuremburg we're laughin, in't we?
Phil	Ah'll be gled tae see the back ae him. Farquhar by name, Farquhar by nature.
Terry	Ah hope his team get gubbed in Germany. (*Raising his fist*) Mon the Bayern! Haud oan. Whitever way ye look at it, the Huns is gonnae win, in't they?
Phil	Whit dae ye mean?
Terry	The Gers an the Germans. Same difference. Baith Huns, in't they?

Phil	Zat right? An whit aboot me? Whit am ah?
Terry	Don't start that again. You're wan ae us. Ah mean, yer a Celtic supporter. That's enough fur me. It's no your fault…
Phil	… It's no ma fault? Look. There's a young boy went tae ma auld school. A few years below me, he wiz. He's gonnae be wearin the hoops. He's oan the books the noo. His first touch is brilliant. He's got vision way beyond his years. He's gonnae be a star. (*Pointing at Terry*) But he's no wan ae yous. (*Tapping his own chest*) He's wan ae us. Same as hauf the team. Same as the manager. Same as maself.
Terry	Aye, but…
Phil	An whit aboot Jackie Ferguson? He's Celtic daft an his da's in the ludge.
Terry	Right, ferr enough. Point taken. We're no like that mob. We're no bigots. We've got an open door.
Phil	Who's we? You don't listen, dae ye?
Terry	Ah am listenin. But aw the guys yer talkin aboot are pure Celtic, in't they? That's whit we've goat in common. Ye must admit, when it comes tae fitba, yer wan ae us. Wan ae the bhoys. The Toi Molloi. When it comes tae fitba, ye cannae see past the Tic.

Phil	Ye widnae be sayin that if ye'd seen Slim Jim Baxter running rings roon the English at Wembley. That wiz fitba.
Terry	Don't wind me up, Phil. There's only wan team in Scotland.
Phil	The SFA wid hiv a joab organising a league if there was only wan team.
Terry	Turn it up, you.
Phil	(Shouting) Ah said, 'The SFA wid hiv a joab organising a league if there was only wan team'.
Terry	(Covering his ears) Awright. Awright. (Holding up his thumbs) Keys. By the way, see that guy ye we're talkin aboot? The wan that went tae your school?
Phil	Aye?
Terry	Whit's his name?
Phil	Kenny Something. Kenny … Dug Leash.
Terry	An ye really think he's Celtic class?
Phil	He's world class.
Terry	That's whit ah mean. Noo cut the cackle an think ae a way we can get tae Lisbon. Come on, ah've got an idea. If we don't come up wae a straight way a daein it, we'll find a crooked wan. Meet me doon at the Roon Toll at six the morra night, an if ye don't hiv a better idea, bring yer maw's nylons. Clean wans.

Phil   **Ah smell trouble.**

[They exit. Lights out]

> 'Belfast 1967: ten years of age and being invisible. 'Keep your head down… say nothing… only brings trouble.' Lisbon 1967: Celtic playing Inter Milan. A sea of green and white on a black and white television – awash with tricolours! A Tommy Gemmell thunderbolt, then Stevie Chalmers… Billy McNeill lifts the European Cup. Celtic won. We won. The world changed. We changed. Invisible no more.'

AIDAN DONALDSON
WRITER

●

> 'It was very easy to be a big Celtic fan in 1967. Every Glaswegian, and beyond, was caught up in the excitement of that massive feather in the cap for Scottish football. As the nation which had given the beautiful game to humanity – wee Renton were world champions in 1888 – Glasgow Celtic's triumph in Lisbon was for every Scot, football lover or not. Lions to a man.'

MARY EDWARD
WRITER

' If you know your history, I know mine. Jack English, husband of Miss Celtic 1966 Kathleen, went to the outside loo in 63 and 84 minutes, as unimaginable as the result itself. He missed the goals, but thrilled his children with a fairytale about eleven Glasgow legends. Three decades later, I interviewed *Cesar* for Glasgow University's newspaper. My print debut, the cutting as treasured now as then. '

PAUL ENGLISH
JOURNALIST

' On 28 September 1966 Glasgow Celtic embarked on what they did not then know would be the greatest journey yet in their history. On 25 May 1967 they played in the European Cup Final. After defeating Inter-Milan 2–1 in Lisbon Jock Stein declared: 'there is not a prouder man on God's Earth than me at this moment… Our objective is always to try to win with style'. '

JIM FERGUSON
POET

' For me, a young part-time pro with Hibs,
Stein was the match-winner. His team-talk
was 'go out and enjoy yourselves, bhoys,'
so they did, ran at the mighty Italian defence
like it was a Sunday afternoon pub-team.
If he had told me I could mix-it with Bertie
Auld, I would have believed him. If he had
told me I was Bertie Auld, I would have
believed him. '

ALISTAIR FINDLAY
WRITER

' It was the best week of my short life. I made my
Confession on the 19th; my Holy Communion
on the 20th; my Confirmation on the 24th
and Celtic won the European Cup on the 25th.
I was the centre of the world that week.
When Tommy Gemmell scored the equaliser
my two big brothers held me up and waved me
about. Could life get any better? '

JEANETTE FINDLAY
ACADEMIC

6

The Women and the Bhoys

The Gorbals

[*Cathy is packing her things. Her friend Theresa is plucking her eyebrows*]

Cathy

Ah never mentioned ma daddy's holy medals, Theresa. That wid've pit the tin lid oan it.

Theresa

Ah don't know why ye bother, Cathy. Yer too honest fur yer ain good. Faither O'Hara gets short shrift fae me. Ah jist confess tae lyin, an leave the rest tae his imagination. The wan time a told the truth ah could hear him breathing like a racehoarse, an he came oot the boax sweatin like a pig. Heaven knows the man's got little enough tae content himself wae. Me waitin ootside the chapel fur you wae thon lime-coloured bri-nylon slacks oan is the highlight ae his week. It's fur his ain protection that ah prefer tae draw a discreet veil ower ma private life.

Cathy Aye. Yer pure discreet, so ye ur. Everybody says that. Your discretion is the talk ae the steamie.

Theresa The priest can pray fur ma soul tae his cassock's through at the knees. Ah don't practice whit he preaches. Why should ah be made tae feel guilty fur the body God gied me?

Cathy Ah've goat enough guilt fur the baith ae us. Ah feel as if ah'm elopin, Theresa. Except instead a wan man, ah'm runnin away wae eleven.

Theresa Aye. Yer team-handed, Cathy.

Cathy Ah'm two faced. Ah cannae crack a light at hame. If ma da knew ah was goin tae Lisbon he'd hit the ceiling.

Theresa How come yer da disnae foally Celtic any mer?

Cathy He stoapped the day ma granda died. Ma da's da, ah'm talkin aboot. He wiz Celtic mad, ma granda. Lived fur a Seterday. Never missed a game. Could reel aff aw the teams fae day wan. It was him that took me tae ma furst game. Hampden in the sun. Celtic seven,

	and Rangers one. Ah'll never furget it. Ma granda wiz 71 at the time. Seven-One. Same as the scoreline. He says he didnae care if he never saw another birthday. That's how daft oan the Celtic he wiz.
Theresa	An did he?
Cathy	He saw another three seasons. Ah wiz at Parkheid wae him the day afore he died. Ah can see him noo, wae his scarf an bunnet, shakin his fist at the referee. Ah wiz amazed that he knew his religion jist bae lookin at him. He says ye could tell bae the way they wore their soacks. Ah mind seein him wance peein intae a boattle. It wiz an Auld Firm game, an he didnae want tae miss a minute. Ah couldnae work oot how he goat his willy intae that wee hole.
Theresa	Ah've seen it done wae a ship, right enough. Ye'd be surprised, Cathy, how many miracles this world has tae offer.
Cathy	Ah wish ma granda wiz alive the day. He'd be in his element. If ma da had had a boay, he'd mibbe still be goin tae the games, but ah think he's always been a wee bit embarrassed aboot me. Thinks ah'm a tomboy. Says its no ladylike tae staun an shout in the Jungle.
Theresa	Ladylike? Haud oan. Ah vernear pit these tweezers through ma eye there. Where is your da fae? Planet Elvis? Ah'll ladylike

	him. Ah'll ladle intae his nuts wae ma slingback.
Cathy	He's dead keen oan the idear a me bein a nun. Thinks it'll book him a grandstand seat in Heaven.
Theresa	So you've tae gie up aw men fur wan man. Did ye no talk tae Faither O'Hara aboot it yet? Ur Sister Bernadette?
Cathy	Ah'm feart they'll laugh.
Theresa	Ah did at furst, but then ah realised ye wur serious. It's nae laughin matter. Yer made fur maternity, Cathy, no eternity. Stoap savin yersel fur Jesus.
Cathy	How no? He's the only man alive ah can trust.
Theresa	They say love heals all wounds.
Cathy	Ah don't care whit they say. Ma mind's made up.
Theresa	Lisbon yer final fling, hen?
Cathy	It's somethin ah widnae miss fur aw the world. Ah don't know if you can understand this, Theresa, but ah feel as if ah'll be closer tae ma granda when ah get there. This last week has brought memories floodin back tae me. Ah feel as if ah'm up oan his shooderz again.
Theresa	Course ah can understand that. It's an upliftin experience. Talkin aboot upliftin experiences, it's gonnae be man-tae-man marking ower there. The odds are

	stacked in oor favour, Cathy. If we cannae get you a lad in Lisbon we should jack it in.
Cathy	Ah am jacking it in as far as men are concerned.
Theresa	Whit? Cos some guy fae Govan let ye doon? Come on. Ye've no played the field yet, an yer away fur an early bath.
Cathy	They're the same the world ower, Theresa. Aw aye, they say they love ye. Tell ye anything, so they will, tae get whit they want. But at the end of the day, yer jist another Saturday tae them.
Theresa	Cathy Boyle! Yer an auld woman afore yer time. But if ye feel that way aboot men then shutting yerself away in a convent isnae gonnae solve anything. The Catholic Church is no exactly at the forefront ae Women's Liberation, ye know. Jist cos yer no happy wae the Sixties disnae mean ye should turn the clock back tae the Middle Ages. If ye think Modern Man's a bugger ye shoulda seen Neolithic man.
Cathy	Did he hiv long hair an a beard?
Theresa	Aye, that's yer man.
Cathy	Ah think ah jist broke up wae him.
Theresa	Then try another type, hen. There's 57 varieties oot there.
Cathy	Ma granda wiz wan ae a kind.

Theresa	See that boss a mine. He's wan ae a kind. A right sleekit bugger. Face wiz trippin him when ah says ah wiz goin tae Lisbon. Ah'm tellin ye Cathy. Boys will be boys, but there's only two kinds a people ah cannae stand. Bigots, an Orange bastards.
Cathy	That's a terrible way tae talk, Theresa Kelly. Whit aboot the ordinary decent Rangers supporter?
Theresa	Ah don't know him. Is he a friend a yours?
Cathy	Ye cannae tar everybody wae the same brush.
Theresa	Ye mean ye cannae put aw yer oranges intae the wan basket?
Cathy	Theresa. How can you be so bitter aboot Protestants when yer losin faith in yer ain religion?
Theresa	Ah'm no losing faith, Cathy. Ah loast it alang wae ma virginity, when ah found oot the earth isnae flat an it can be made tae move. An ah've nothing against Protestants. It's bigots ah cannae stand.
Cathy	There's bigots oan baith sides.
Theresa	Ah know that. An as far as ah'm concerned the Orange Lodge an the Vatican can go tae Hell oan the same banana boat. The only Men's Club ah've goat time fur is Celtic.

Cathy	Me tae. Celtic are the only men ye can trust. They'll no let ye doon. (*Finishes her hair*) Right. Whit dae ye think? Dae ah look like a tomboy, Theresa?
Theresa	Naw. Ye look like Dusty Springfield. Pure immaculate. Haud oan a minute, there's jist wan hair oot ae place.
Cathy	It's no too severe?
Theresa	Mer sophisticated. Ye look as if ye've goat a few bob. Much spendin money ur ye takin?
Cathy	A tenner.
Theresa	Ur you kiddin? Whit ur ye gonnae live aff ae? Are you goin tae the game ur goin oan the game?
Cathy	It's enough tae get by oan. Everythin's paid fur an the drink' s meant tae be dirt cheap.
Theresa	Look. Ah'll gie ye a bung. It's me that'll get the blame if ye come back like a whippet.
Cathy	Ah wiz thinkin ae goin oan a diet anyway.
Theresa	It's exercise ye need, hen.
Cathy	Ah can jist picture whit ye've goat in mind.
Theresa	Ah wiz actually thinkin ae hirin bikes in Lisbon an daein a wee bit a sightseeing.
Cathy	I'll settle fur sun, sea an sand.

Theresa	Wae a tenner ye'll hiv tae. Everythin else costs money.
Cathy	Dae ye think ah wiz daft tae gie up ma joab?
Theresa	No way. Ye cannae ride two hoarses wae wan arse, Cathy. It wiz either Celtic ur Marks an Sparks. Anyhow, there's plenty a joabs nooadays. An if all else fails ye can always get doon oan yer knees an pray tae St Michael, seen ye've yer heart set oan bein a nun. A nun by Christ! Ye'd be better aff as a nurse. Aw they young doctors, an ye could still see the Celtic oan a Seterday.
Cathy	Ah want tae live in a safe hoose. Wae people ah love, an that love me.
Theresa	So dae ah. But ye don't need tae hide yerself away in a convent tae get it. Ah'm no gonnae end up like ma maw. Ah'm tellin ye, Cathy, ah want somethin better than she goat. Hosin doon tramcars. Chained tae a man that carries coal bae day an gets carted hame at night. Stuck up a smelly close. No fur me. Ah'm gonnae marry money. Get a wee hoose doon at the coast. Put something by fur ma auld age. Big stroang sons tae look efter me. Ronnie, Jimmy, Tommy, Bobby, Billy, John, Steve, Bertie.
Cathy	Names tae conjure wae. Ah still cannae believe we're goin tae see the Celtic, Theresa. It's a wance in a lifetime

experience. An we're gettin a holiday oot ae it intae the bargain. It's a dream come true. Ah've no been any further than Saltcoats.

Theresa	You've no been the length of a duffelcoat.
Cathy	Ah'd walk a million miles for Celtic, but.
Theresa	Ye'd hiv tae before ye could get intae they bloody itsy-bitsy costumes ye lifted.
Cathy	Brown is beautiful.
Theresa	So is green an white. Ah'm tellin ye, Cathy. Ah'll be runnin oantae the pitch wae nothin bit a scarf roon me if the Tic lift that cup. Ah swear it.
Cathy	Ah'll be at yer back wae a tammy.
Theresa	Ye'll hiv 10,000 guys in front ae ye.
Cathy	Lisbon, Theresa. It's gonnae separate the men fae the bhoys, isn't it?
Theresa	Let's hope it disnae separate the women fae the boys, eh?

[lights out]

'Classic drama was played out in Lisbon –
protagonist, antagonist, cynicism, romance,
contrast, conflict, setback and revival – but a
longer distinction should be prized too. Between
1956 and 1967 the European Cup had been
confined to the Latin triangle of Spain, Portugal
and Italy. From 1967 it would remain in Northern
Europe for 17 of the next 18 years. Big Jock
commanded a radical changing of the guard.'

RODDY FORSYTH
JOURNALIST

'Blue blazer. Pencil. Tie. The telly is awash with
sea birds, caked with crude and dying in the
living room. Torrey Canyon. Wherever that is.
Stop crying you, godsake it's only birds.
Sergeant Pepper will be broadcast on the telly
one day soon, live and in colour. Miracles.
Switch before the football, hen. Lisbon,
wherever that is. Finish the homework, mind.
Straight to bed after the Queen.'

JANICE GALLOWAY
WRITER

> If you can have such a thing, it's my favourite year. My son was born in February 1967, Sergeant Pepper, the album that changed the musical world was launched. And of course the victory that changed Celtic Football Club happened. My son had actually attended the early rounds in utero. His birth precluded my attendance in Lisbon although we both managed Seville. We'll be there next time!

JOHN GILLEN
TRADE UNIONIST

> On the other side of Hadrian's Wall, in a southern spot called the North, older fans still say, 'We were first', which suits them. Most get plenty of practise at being one-eyed. No glorious denial of the tripletta. No death of Herrera's La Grande Inter. No Scottish victory over the all-Italian *catenaccio*. Busby, Best, Charlton, Kidd. Ex-Celt Crerand. Foragers, explorers. It feels good to be the first.

RODGE GLASS
WRITER

'My father was a home and away guy for a time. Imagine his surprise when the Celtic reached Lisbon in the week his third child was due. Imagine his dilemma. Should I stay or should I go? And his ire when the wean was born late. He's a better man than me. I'd have gone to Portugal! Yet I should be grateful. I am that third child. '

TONY HAMILTON
CEO OF CELTIC FC FOUNDATION

●

'The Estádio Nacional – Lisbon had always been part of my life. I knew it intimately from a lifetime of watching that fabled game, poring over photos, reading the biographies and hearing the stories: '41 attempts on goal Celtic had that night!'

I finally got there in 2007. To my astonishment the Lions were there, for their 40th Anniversary. Walked on the pitch with the players. Hugely emotional... '

PATRICK HARKINS
FILMMAKER

7

Hail! Hail!

[*Phil and Terry are busking – 'Halfway to Paradise'. Phil is wearing a T-shirt that says 'Lisbon or Bust'. Terry is wearing one that says 'Bust'. Theresa walks on and drops a coin in the boys' green and white bunnet*]

Theresa   Dae yez no know 'Silence is Golden'?

[*She walks off. Phil and Terry stop singing and look at one another, then down at the bunnet. Phil picks it up and starts counting the contents*]

Terry   Much hiv we made?

Phil   Seven an six.

Terry   That'll get us as far as Gretna Green.

Phil   Glesca Green, mer like. This is nae use. (*Handing Terry the bunnet*) Here, haud this.

Terry	Where are ye goin?
Phil	Tae buy a per a nylons.
Terry	Naw, haud oan. Ah've a better idea. Let's take coal tae Newcastle.
Phil	Whit?
Terry	How many Celtic supporters are goin tae Lisbon?
Phil	Hunnerz an thousands. Minus two.
Terry	Plus two, if we play wur cards right. When in Rome, an aw that.
Phil	Whit are ye oan aboot? It's Lisbon we want tae get tae.
Terry	That's whit ah'm sayin. We should save oor voices fur the game an use wur heids fur a change.
Phil	Yer no gonnae get us intae a fight, ur ye?
Terry	Naw. Listen. Whit can ye buy at Parkhead that ye cannae get in Portugal?
Phil	Cauld pies? Bovril?
Terry	Whit else?
Phil	Ah give in.
Terry	That's your problem, Phil. Ye give in too easy. There's customers galore makin there way tae Lisbon.
Phil	Supporters, Terry. Supporters.
Terry	Every supporter is a customer, Phil. It's the first law of economics.

Phil	So whit ur we sellin?
Terry	Sweeties, Phil. Awz we need is a big cargo a spearmint an macaroon an we've got it made.
Phil	An where'll we get a big cargo a spearmint an macaroon in a hurry?
Terry	Spinetti's. Big Tony'll gie us money up front if we promise him a hefty profit. He's goat a nose fur business.
Phil	He's also goat a golf club an a big Alsatian. We'd better sell or no return, ur we'll be chewin oor arses an thinkin it's chewing-gum. Big Tony's no a man tae cross.
Terry	It's a cakewalk, Phil. Aw they Celtic fans cryin oot fur a taste a paradise, feelin homesick, an me an you coinin it wae the goodies. We cannae lose.
Phil	Ah suppose if the worst comes tae the worst we'll come back weighin twinty stone apiece. Tony'll never recognise us. An if he diz, we'll hiv nae teeth left fur him tae knoack oot.
Terry	An it's better than gettin caught bae big Farquhar wearin a nylon ower yer napper, in't it? Come on, we'll fire doon tae Maryhill an pit it tae Tony. This could be oor meal ticket tae Lisbon.

[Exit]

'It was the time I realised men could become gods. They looked it, in the hoops, the white shorts, the white socks. They flew over the pitch, swooping into the clear blue sky, taking thousands of hearts, maybe millions, with them. Yet their faces were straight from the Glasgow streets. And writers like Hugh McIlvanney whispered sporting greatness begets brilliant writing, inspiring a lost ten year old.'

CHRIS HART
SENIOR LECTURER IN MENTAL HEALTH

'I was on the backshift at the *Express*. The pre-match rituals were well underway in the Press Bar downstairs. This was the big one, there could be no bigger story that night. The news desks were on edge. Then the phone rang with a tip off that a nuclear submarine at Faslane was leaking radiation. Who got the assignment? Me, the only Celtic supporter in the office.'

BILL HEANEY
JOURNALIST AND WRITER

' In 2003, a friend and I were fortunate enough to explore the Estádio Nacional and have a kickabout on the hallowed turf. On that sunny afternoon it was no longer summer 2003; it was May 1967. We relived key moments and lifted the big cup – achievements permanently etched in the minds of every Celtic fan. We recreated history, we felt the magic and we lived the dream.

AARON HEPBURN
FAN

●

' Who else has 1967 as a pin number? Who else displays his Lions photograph before wedding snaps or kids in school uniform are even unpacked? Who else sees a glint of himself in the shyness of their smiles and the carefulness of their poses, yet puts them on a glorious pedestal higher than God, Dylan, or Football itself. You too? Meet my husband. He's romantic like that.

ALISON IRVINE
WRITER

Over-excitable and asthmatic, I had opted for a behind the couch place. Two brothers and a dad moved swift – telly images lit up the rosary space. 'Say another decade hen, and keep rattling they bloody beads.' The Estádio Nacional shone into our Glenburn home. Foreign voices, Scottish hoops swelling in song. Gemmell, Chalmers and it's going to be a long, beautiful night of never walking alone.

LINDA JACKSON
SINGER

Lisbon: the very name sends a shiver down my spine. I was a five-year-old queuing up to have a photograph taken with Billy McNeill and the cup. Before my turn they ran out of film. I cried the whole way home. My uncle Jim, made redundant a week before the final, used his dundy money to take his best pal to Lisbon. There goes that shiver again.

ANDREW JAMIESON
FAN

8

The Road to Lisbon

Glasgow Airport and Dover Ferry

[*Cathy and Theresa boarding for Lisbon*]

Theresa   There'll be mer talent ower there than
             there is in the Celtic dressing room.
             Some ae they Italians are pure dishy. An
             they Portuguese. The dark flashin eyes.
             We'll be able tae pick an mix, Cathy.

Cathy   Aw aye. Eyes meetin acroass a crowded
             terracin. Somethin that could last
             forever.

Theresa   It can happen anywhere, hen.

Cathy   Ah don't believe in love at first sight. It
             disnae happen that way. A holiday
             romance is like an ice-lolly. It's nice while
             it lasts but it disnae last long.

Theresa	Well. Ah hope you meet a man in Lisbon that changes yer mind an saves ye fae a life behind closed doors.
Cathy	He'd need tae walk oan watter.
Theresa	Maist Celtic supporters wid, tae get tae Lisbon.

[*Light shifts to Phil and Terry, draped in green and white, and wheeling a cart laden with luggage*]

Terry	Dover, Phil ma man. We're aw there bar the shoutin.
Phil	The shoutin'll start any minute. How are we going tae get this lot through customs?
Terry	Nae tother a baw. They'll think we're a pair a stylish bastards wae stacks a claes, an wave us through. We'll sell the cases efter we've sold the merchandise. It'll go sweet as a nut, Phil.
Phil	Ah wish ah had your faith.
Terry	So dae ah. Ye widnae wind me up so much if ye had ma faith.
Phil	How long is it since you were in a chapel, ya big hypocrite?
Terry	It's no long since a wiz oan the roof ae wan.
Phil	Stealin lead. Sacrilege, that wiz.
Terry	Ah did it fur the Bhoys, didn't ah? It wiznae easy. That Gorbals is a dodgy

pitch. See when ah wiz up there, ah drapped ma hat. Ah says tae wee Davie, jump doon an get it an ah'll keep the L.O. So doon he goes. Next minute he comes back wae the hat, an it's wringin. 'Where wiz it?', ah says. 'In the urinal'. 'Where's that?' 'How the fuck dae ah know', he says. 'Ah'm no a Catholic'.

Phil   Heard it.

Terry   Ah'm no surprised. It wiz wringin.

Phil   Ah don't know how ye can live yer life withoot morals.

Terry   Ah believe in Celtic. Faithful through an through. Ah support the Tic, an the Tic support me.

Phil   That's right. Ye get everythin oan tic. Including the spearmint an the macaroon. You're a practisin chancer.

Terry   It's allowed.

[*Light shifts to Father O'Hara and Inspector Farquhar. A teddy bear peeks out from Farquhar's holdall*]

Father O'Hara   (*Looking Farquhar up and down*) Excuse me? Are you sure you're in the right queue?

Farquhar   Unfortunately.

Father O'Hara   You're gonnae be as welcome as a fart in a spacesuit. (*Checking his own ticket, then looking over Farquhar's shoulder at his*) Looks like we're sittin thegither, tae. It's no your day, is it?

Farquhar	It's no ma season.
Father O'Hara	Ah'll dae ma best tae cheer ye up.
Farquhar	Ah'm sure ye will.
Father O'Hara	Did ye hear the latest wan aboot John Greig?
Farquhar	I'm afraid not.
Father O'Hara	Big John, right. He's ower in Lisbon, right.
Farquhar	Whit's John Greig doing in Lisbon?
Father O'Hara	It's a joke.
Farquhar	Yer no kidding.
Father O'Hara	Anyhow, John Greig, right, ower in Lisbon – fur the purposes ae this joke – sittin in this bar, an this big bull comes in. Greig stauns up an says, 'Dae you want a game a heidy-kick?' The bull says 'Naw.' Big John says 'How no?' The bull says, 'Ah'm no wearin shin guards.'

[Farquhar is not amused. Back to Phil and Terry, who are joined by a youthful Danny]

Danny	Hey lads. Are ye goin to the game, by any chance?
Terry	Naw, we're jist goin tae a fancy-dress party as Robin Hood's Merry Men.
Danny	Dae yez mind if I tag along? I'm on ma own.
Phil	Hiv ye goat plenty a money oan ye?
Danny	Why do I feel like Pinocchio all of a

	sudden? Aye, I've got money. Plenty for maself. What of it?
Terry	What of it? If money's of no importance tae ye, could ye sling a few quid in oor direction?
Danny	And what do I get in return?
Terry	The pleasure ae oor company. Share an share alike.
Danny	No thanks, I'll manage on me own.
Terry	Haud oan. Dae ye fancy a packet a spearmint ur a bar a macaroon?
Danny	How much?
Phil	Shilling a shout.
Danny	Two bob for a bit a chewing-gum and a macaroon bar? Yez are a pair of Robin Hoods right enough. Yez would have the skin off me arse if ah stayed in yer company.
Terry	We'll see ye oan the ferry, then.
Danny	Through a telescope, if yer lucky.

[*Danny goes off*]

Terry	Dae ye think we wur a wee bit oot ae order, there?
Phil	Definitely.
Terry	Ah feel pure ignorant fur the guy. He's wan ae us, ye know whit ah mean?
Phil	But we're Scottish an he's Irish.

Terry	Gie it a bye, you. Ye know whit ah mean. The guy wiz wan ae us. But did ye see the size ae the turn-ups in his troosers? Ye could smuggle all sorts a stuff through customs wae thaim oan. An they boots were made fur walkin, wur they no? He's aboot ten year oot a date, that guy.
Phil	So are some a these macaroon bars, judgin bae the wrappers.
Terry	They're hermless. It's jist sugar an spice. No too good fur the auld Cowdenbeath, but apart fae that, they're brand new.
Phil	Naw they're no. The prices are in Roman numerals.
Terry	There's nothing wrang wae nostalgia.
Phil	Ye mean neuralgia?
Terry	Talkin a which. Ah heard watchin they Italians is like pullin teeth.
Phil	Jist as well Jim Craig's a dentist. It'll be a wee hame fae hame fur him.
Terry	An wae this lot we'll keep his profession in business fur a good few years. Edge up. Ah spy a few customers.
Phil	Erri spearmint an a macaroon!
Terry	If yer no fast, yer last!
Phil	Come an get it! Stick in tae ye stick oot!
Terry	Yer money ur yer teeth!

Phil   If ye cannae get a boat, come an get a
        choo-choo!

        [Lights out]

Half Time

9

Lost in Lisbon

[*Phil and Terry have just set up camp outside Lisbon*]

Phil
: Well seen you were never a Boy Scout. Four hours tae pitch a tent. Ah telt ye we should hiv goat an apartment.

Terry
: Whit wae? We've barely goat drinkin money. Besides, the outdoor life is good fur ye. Pits herz oan yir tits.

Phil
: It's food in ma stomach ah want.

Terry
: It's hope in yer heart ye need.

Phil
: Ah've goat that, awright. Ah've goat a sweetness inside, Terry. We're gonnae win. Wae the likes ae Cesar, Jinky an Wispy, how can we lose?

Terry
: We cannae. We've won everythin there is tae win, except Wimbledon. The European Cup'll be the icin oan the cake.

Phil	Don't mention cake. Ma teeth are achin. Whit a journey. Ah telt ye we shoulda flew. That bus wiz like a buckin bronco.
Terry	You watch yer language. An whit dae ye expect fur sixteen pound return? That widnae hiv goat us a flight tae the Isle a Man. We shifted a bit of cargo, Phil. That's the main thing. Paid oor way, that did. Part ae it, any road. There's nothin like havin captive customers.
Phil	Passengers.
Terry	That's what ah said. Customers. That bus wiz a joke right enough, though. Ah'm sure ah saw the driver pedallin.
Phil	Come oan we'll find wan a they Bureau de Chancers an change wur money.
Terry	Ah wish we could change fivers intae tenners.
Phil	Ah wish ah could change ma drawers. It's standin room only wae these strides. Aw that travellin an nothin tae eat but spearmint an macaroon. Ah've been mer than regular since we croassed the Channel. When you said they swadgers wid help us tae work oor passages ah didnae think ye had this in mind.
Terry	Did ye no bring a change a claes wae ye, ya manky bastard?
Phil	Where wid ah hiv put them? The cases wur wall tae wall spearmint an macaroon.

Terry	Well. There's nae flies oan me. Ah had a couple a T-shirts an a sloppy Joe rolled up wae the tent.
Phil	Ah wish we'd broat two tents. There's nae room fur us in there. You were talkin aboot talent tae. Who could we bring back tae that midden?
Terry	That tent's gonnae be a hive of activity, ma man.
Phil	That tent's gonnae be a den of iniquity.
Terry	It's a two-man tent, but it sleeps four, know whit ah mean?
Phil	Aye, four dwarves wae nae sense a smell. In fact, four dwarves wae nae sense. Whit makes ye think a woman in her right mind wid go near a dive like that.
Terry	Put it this way, Phil. It's exotic, innit. Fry's Turkish Delight, an aw that? Bring her to my tent, know whit ah mean? The burdz love that kinna hing. Wee bit a danger. Wee bit a romance.
Phil	Wee bit a spearmint an macaroon.
Terry	Could be. Look at us Phil, the outlook's sunny …
Phil	… Two ton a macaroon, but no fuckin money.

[Lights out]

" Big number. It's the year of my brother Gregory's birth – without whom, no musical partner, no Hue And Cry. But it's also the year my Dad made a fateful decision. £600 saved for Lisbon – but then my Mum's dream Blairhill house is on the market, requiring as a deposit… No greater love could a Coatbridge man have for his wife. My dad's gone. But she's still there. "

PAT KANE
MUSICIAN AND WRITER

" A victory for localism and internationalism: localism that is irreducible to sectarianism or ethnicity in that those born in a 30 miles radius from the stadium were already a product of transnational migration and dislocation and it didn't matter what religion they were; international in that they inspired all of us. You'll Never Walk Alone: we will find community in our capacity to unite with all people. "

AARON KELLY
ACADEMIC

'Came out the subway and dived into a pub to see the goals on the nine o'clock news. Standing with a big excited grin to see this already famous event. Noticed some folk seemed to be watching me watching the news, and nobody watching the telly itself. Shot back out into the night as soon as it was over. Turned out I'd gone into Willie Woodburn's Bar.'

TOM LEONARD
POET

'My tenth birthday, three days before the Final, attending St Mary's RC primary in the mining town of Worksop. Forty-one boys and girls in class. Only three have an allegiance to Celtic and understand the significance of the game to be played that tea-time. Catenaccio unlocked, total football. One year later, a rash of Best football boots and Man Utd duffle bags – forgive them, they don't understand.'

JIM LISTER
PRODUCER

10

The Tally and the Toaly

[*Hector Farquhar, in shirtsleeves, with his trouser legs rolled up, meets Donaldo, an Inter Milan fan*]

Farquhar   If another person blesses me I'm going to go Radio Rental. This is worse than being in a bloody bookies. Hello, hello, hello. As the stutterin sergeant said, 'I spy, with my little eye something beginning with … "I".' It's a big eye-tie. Afternoon, Sir.

Donaldo   Sorry?

Farquhar   No speaky English? No need to apologise, Sir. If we British taught all you people our language we wouldn't have a country left to call our own, would we? Going to the game, are we? Yous were on the wrong side during the last war, but yer the lesser of two evils. Ah

hope your team whack they paddies,
either that, or the ground opens up and
swallows the lot of you. (*Tipping his hat*)
Au revoir, Mussolini.

[*Farquhar walks off laughing*]

Donaldo   Whit an arsehole.

[He exits]

‟ Ten stitches after one bad tackle in a one on one on ash. Then 15 of us in the school gym, opened specially. Then ten bob from Mr Murphy outside the Cartvale Bar on the way home. But up to No. 25 because our maw said we had to give it back. Then three brothers in one room laughing all night. That makes 67. More than a number. „

HUGH MACDONALD
JOURNALIST

‟ When wee, I was jealous of fellow ginger Jinky Johnstone. I thought my dad loved him more than me. I knew I made my dad proud tho' when directing Willy Maley and Ian Auld's *The Lions of Lisbon* at Glasgow Pavilion. A box office hit celebrating Celtic's victory where the likes of wee Jinky showed some bottle, went full throttle, enough to make us all love him. „

LIBBY McARTHUR
ACTOR, WRITER, DIRECTOR

'Life began on the 25th of May 1967.
The panorama of invading Celtic fans
sketched the canvas of my soon to be world,
a palette of green and white embroidering the
Portuguese skyline in the flecks of an impregnate
joy. As the European Cup advanced
heavenwards, in the arms of a colossus,
I am twinkling in its reflection, a child born
nine months and three days later. '

MARGOT McCUAIG
FILMMAKER, CHILD OF LISBON

'The sun seemed brighter then, when the
green and white looked more beautiful
than a love affair in its early glow.
Because a man who was moulded underground,
guided a group of young Scots, above the
clouds, beyond the stars to immortality. Telling
us we are here, we matter. Those who came
before, and those yet to come. Hail the Lisbon
Lions, Hail the great Jock Stein. '

MARTIN McCARDIE
ACTOR, WRITER, DIRECTOR

" My dad and his mates in Lisbon. Locals hid
their passports to stop them leaving.
They partied together for weeks, floating
back home on euphoria and wine. My dad:
the part-time mythologiser, but full-time fan.
I believe it still. Story-telling in the DNA?
I wrote a play about Johnny Thomson.
Dad never lived to see it. A circle unbroken.
The circle of a crest. That's no myth. "

BRIAN McGEACHAN
WRITER

" I was proud and privileged to see that
winning goal and celebrate one of the giant
moments of Scottish, British and European
football. The Lions were a team of outstanding
talent, skill and courage. I was delighted to
meet some of the players decades later in my
political life. Working class boys, a credit to
their club and country. We can enjoy the
memories and still dream. "

HENRY McLEISH
FORMER FIRST MINISTER OF SCOTLAND

11

Going to the Chapel

[*Father O'Hara appears, consulting a street map*]

Father O'Hara Aw, ma poor toes. The ball never gets tired, but your feet dae. These Hush Puppies are meltin. Ah wunner how much they Italians are oan a man? Too much ah'll bet. Then there'll be a bonus if they win. Some hope. Ah wunner how priests are treated in Italy? A damn sight better than the Gorbals, that's for sure. It's the Holy Father's home pitch, efter aw. Let's see noo. The sun sets in the west. That's no much help when it's directly overhead. Must be twelve o'clock. Ah'm due to be fed and watered. Never mind Fatima! Where am ah?

[*As he points, Danny appears from the same direction*]

Danny	Hello, Father. Do you speak English?
Father O'Hara	A little, my son. You could say it's a second language. I'm from Glasgow.
Danny	I'm from Ireland. Daniel Gallagher. English is my second language too.
Father O'Hara	Ah'm Father O'Hara. Pleased to meet you, Daniel. Which part of Ireland are you from?
Danny	Donegal. Buncrana. Do you know it?
Father O'Hara	Do I know it? Half my flock are from there or thereabouts.
Danny	It's a small world.
Father O'Hara	And yet you can still get lost in it.
Danny	Are ye lost, then, Father?
Father O'Hara	Not spiritually. Just geographically. I'm a stranger in paradise. Lisbon is a labyrinth, Daniel. There's a chapel on every corner, so it's hard to get your bearings. In Glasgow, you can use the pubs as a compass. Here it's rather more difficult.
Danny	Where are you trying to get to?
Father O'Hara	Fatima, ultimately. Would you like to join me?
Danny	I'd love to, Father. But to tell you the truth, ma throat's as dry as dust wi walkin in the sun. I'm dyin for a drink.
Father O'Hara	Do you know, so am I. Do you mind if I join you?

Danny	I don't want to be takin ye out of yer way, Father.
Father O'Hara	Not at all. Ah'm always ready to lend spiritual assistance to wan ae the faithful. Ah passed a wee taverna about a hundred yards back up that road that looked particularly enticing.
Danny	Are ye sure?
Father O'Hara	Sure I'm sure. Bread and wine, Daniel, are good for the spirit. Especially wine.
Danny	Lead the way, Father.
Father O'Hara	Tell me about the priests in Ireland, Daniel. Are they well looked after?

[They exit]

'My father and his brothers made out of Stein
A graven image;
Hewn from the shaft of a Lanarkshire coalmine,
A blackened messiah
As children we asked God to deliver him
From devils incarnate

To me though, he was Moses, leading
His people out of captivity
And in Lisbon where fascism was soon to die
Amidst carnations
His team of lions wrought a different kind
of revolution.'

KEVIN McKENNA
JOURNALIST

‘ The crowd went crazy. I ran round the backcourt celebrating. I memorised the team sheet like a litany. Years later, I met Ian Auld, full of stories. We wrote a play for the 25th anniversary. It was real teamwork. We made a great double act. Then we lost touch. Ian passed away. I have a season ticket for the Lisbon Lions Stand today. The story goes on. ’

WILLY MALEY
ACADEMIC, WRITER

‘ I was once in the same room as Billy McNeill but I was too starstruck to introduce myself and shake his hand. My first Celtic game was the centenary Cup Final; my childhood full of stories of the Lisbon Lions. I couldn't believe he was just standing there like a regular mortal. McNeill really is like Caesar: a colossal figure from history. I still regret my shyness. ’

IAIN MALONEY
WRITER

12

The Law of the Jungle

[Phil and Terry are hungover]

Phil	Is there laces oan ma heid, Terry? Ah feel as if somedy's been playin keepy-up wae it.
Terry	Mine's is stuck in the junction between the bar an the post, Phil.
Phil	That wine must hiv been aff. How did we get here?
Terry	Ah don't know. When we left that wee bar, visibility wiz doon tae ten pints.
Phil	Aye, ah think the fifth boattle musta been a bad yin. It wiz years auld. It's a wunner we're still alive.

| Terry | Ye know, ah hid the weirdest dream. Ah wiz at the bar ae this wee taverna, trying tae pass embassy coupons aff as escudos, when who taps me oan the shooder, but big Farquhar. |
| Phil | Ah telt ye they macaroon bars wur aff. |

[*Enter Inspector Farquhar*]

Terry	Speak ae the Devil.
Phil	(*Rubbing his eyes*) Am ah seeing things?
Farquhar	Could I see your tickets, lads?
Terry	They're in oor tent.
Farquhar	Oh, rent-a-tent, is it? A pair of your flared trousers held down by a couple of clothespins, no doubt. I hope you're not camping on private property?
Phil	Naw, we're oan the beach.
Farquhar	That explains the tidemark on yer neck, Divers.
Phil	We're jist gaun there noo, in fact.
Terry	Aye. We're gonnae get lost.
Farquhar	You know what they say. If you get lost, ask a policeman.
Phil	How did you get here?
Farquhar	Have ye never heard of the long arm of

	the law? It's got long legs too. I'll see yous to your tent.
Terry	Naw thanks, two's company an aw that.
Farquhar	Ah thoat you liked the roar ae the crowd, Docherty? There's safety in numbers. Allow me to give you an escort.
Terry	A wee Hillman Imp wid dae us.
Farquhar	Pardon?
Terry	Ah'd like wan, but it has tae come straight fae the Queen.
Farquhar	You've been too long in the sun, lad.
Terry	Ah lie longer in the mornins. The teacher said ah wiz big fur ma height.
Farquhar	You need some air about your head.
Phil	Come on, Terry. It's cool in the tent. Ye can have a wee siesta.
Terry	Aye, then ah'm gaun fur a sleep.
Farquhar	What's all that?
Phil	Spearmint an macaroon.
Terry	Special offer, tanner a time.
Farquhar	Bribing a police officer is a serious crime. Have you got a license to sell this stuff? I'll be wantin to see it.

Phil	It's no fur sale, inspector. It's fur personal use.
Terry	Aye. Ah wiz only kiddin aboot the tanner.
Phil	We'd better be goin.
Farquhar	Don't worry, lads. As long as I'm here, you'll never walk alone. I'll be bringing up the rear.
Phil	Aye, in a wheelbarra.
Farquhar	Say that again?
Phil	Look, we're in a hurry.
Terry	Nae offence.
Farquhar	I've seen your charge sheet, Docherty.
Terry	I'm straight noo.
Farquhar	You're as straight as a spiral staircase. If I remember rightly, the first time I booked you, it was for hittin a guy with a claespole.
Terry	Ah had tae. He wiz runnin away. It wiz the only thing that wid reach him.
Phil	(*Checks watch*) Christ. Is that the time already? We'll catch you on the rebound. Keep up the good work.

[*They exit*]

Farquhar   Okay. On yous go. Run along. But
           remember, Big Farquhar is watching you.
           Wan false move and you'll be wheeched
           back to Glasgow so fast your feet won't
           touch the ground. And you'll need the
           fire brigade to get my boot out yer arse.

[He exits. Lights out]

> We didnae have the money. Six of us in two bedrooms. But he still went: waistcoated suit, hair margarined wi Stork. On the victorious supporters' bus back home, he burned his hand wi a fag. Drunk senseless, slumped sideways, he didnae feel his skin sizzle and singe. Burnt to the bone. A Capstan Full Strength stigmata. He didnae work for a month. We didnae have the money.

LAURA MARNEY
WRITER

> As a life-long Hibee I can well remember May 1967. Jock Stein had begun rebuilding Hibs in the early 1960s. We weren't pleased when he returned to Celtic because we knew he was destined for greatness. I watched the game on my mother's TV. It had a bigger screen than mine. At the final whistle I made my way up Dublin Street to celebrate in Milne's Bar.

SANDY MOFFAT
ARTIST

' Stevie was in Lisbon and I, a man of five,
was in Stobhill isolation unit, eczema still
mysterious. Dad played with Chalmers at
Brunswick Boys Club, Struth signed maternal
grampa Trotter for Rangers, Chapman took
him to Arsenal. But when nurse let me oot,
I dribbled the baw at the blocks on Rye Road,
Barmulloch so I too could score the winner.
Everybody wanted to be Stevie. '

CRAIG MUNRO
ACTOR

' What I remember was I kept meeting old
school friends (I had only left the year before).
As most of us were Catholics and it was a
holiday of obligation we headed for a church.
There were a few old ladies in black, a few rich
people with seats inside the altar area, and
masses of Celtic fans with scarves and banners.
The locals were totally bemused. '

DES MURPHY
FORMER TEACHER

> The privilege of being born in the same year as The Lisbon Lions Victory is a badge of pride that both my dad and in turn myself will wear with honour until the end of our lives. My own children now carry the knowledge with them and I expect it to pass down the line. '67 will never be forgotten. It's carved in history forever. Hail Hail.

MICHAEL NARDONE
ACTOR

> At my father's knee I learned that Celtic were the club founded by us: the poor Irish. They were our team. From afar, I observed a scene that fulfilled the dreams of millions. 'Nanny' Robinson's television set flickered, as eleven titans did battle on my behalf. The unconquerable Lions answered the fervent prayers of an eight-year old boy. On that day, I was proud to be alive.

GED O'BRIEN
TEACHER, WRITER

13

A Couple of Chancers

[*Cathy and Theresa enter, wearing sunglasses and floppy hats, Celtic jerseys, and hot pants*]

Theresa   Well, Cathy, whit dae ye think?

Cathy   Paradise, Theresa. Pure paradise.

Theresa   Feel the heat in that sun. Melt ye, so it wid. Rid roastin.

Cathy   Ah burn awfy easy. Ah'd better watch maself. Ah want bronzed, no braised.

Theresa   Here. Pit some mer ae this lotion oan. You should be in yer element. Jesus wants ye fur a sunbeam.

Cathy   Very funny. Ah'm drouth, Theresa. Hiv ye any ae that ginger left?

Theresa   Jist a moothfy.

Cathy	See us it here. (*She drinks*) Pure paradise.
Theresa	Ah'm tellin ye, Cathy. Ye shoulda taen ma advice an went oan the pill. Ye'd think ye'd never heard ae women's lib.
Cathy	(*Handing the bottle back to Theresa*) Ah'm no that kinna lassie.
Theresa	(*Holding the bottle up*) Well think aboot it. Long and hard.
Cathy	That flight wiz a bit hairy, wiz it no? Aw they men getting tanked up. The smell a drink wiz gien me the boke.
Theresa	See when that guy organised a whip-roon fur the pilot. Ah vernear died. Pure brassneck. Glasgow guys. Ye cannae take them anywhere.
Cathy	But they go jist the same.
Theresa	Some ae the locals are gorgeous, though, ye must admit.
Cathy	This place is gorgeous.
Theresa	Absolutely magic. Aw we need noo is tae meet a couple a dreamboats and sail away intae the distance. Haud oan, ah see ship smoke oan the horizon.

[*Phil and Terry appear, puffing away*]

Phil	Imagine that big Farquhar bein here …

Terry	... Edge up, Phil! There's a couple a crackers waitin tae be pulled.
Phil	Mine's the blonde.
Terry	Can ye fight?
Phil	Ah prefer mousey browns anyhow.
Terry	Whit's ma hair like?
Phil	Minted. Noo act natural. Don't be too obvious.
Terry	Watch me. Ye might learn something. (*Adjusting his trousers, and swaggering forward*) Whit are ye fond ae, blondie?
Theresa	No you, fur a kick-aff.
Phil	Play it laid back, Terry, yer bein too blatant.
Terry	(*to Phil*) Ah know whit ah'm daein. It's a canter.
Phil	(*to Terry*) It's keech, Terry. Ye'll make them bolt. Yer patter's gonnae get us plums.
Terry	Ma patter's gonnae get us peaches. (*To Theresa*) Ma name's Terry, but you can call me lover-boy.
Theresa	Ah'll call ye bovver-boy. Are you oot oan bail?
Terry	She's a right gallus Alice, Phil. (*To Theresa*) Yer mammy keeps ye nice.

Theresa	Diz your mammy know yer oot?
Phil	She's fly tae ye, Terry. Ah'm gonnae make a move fur her pal afore you snooker me. (*To Cathy*) Hello, ah'm Phil.
Cathy	Ye look it. Ah'm Cathy. This is Theresa.
Terry	How we doin, Theresa? Ah'm Terry. You're no called Terry fur short, ur ye? This could be fate.
Theresa	Fate can be fatal.
Phil	How long hiv ye been in Lisbon, Cathy?
Cathy	This is wur second day. We flew in yesterday.
Phil	We're campin.
Theresa	(*under her breath*) The last ae the big spenders.
Terry	(*to Phil*) Did she say somethin aboot suspenders?
Phil	Zip it. (*to Cathy*) Where are you two parked?
Cathy	We're stayin at a hotel. It's pure crackin.
Terry	(*out of the corner of his mouth, to Phil*) Ya dancer. We've knocked it oaff here. Keep gaun. Yer playin a blinder.
Phil	(*to Terry*) Get aff ma back, then. Yer like a bull in heat. (*To Cathy*) Hiv yez goat tickets?

Cathy	Aye. Everythin's paid fur. It's a package deal.
Terry	(*to Phil*) It's a package deal aw right. We'll move in wae them, leave them greetin fur mer, an snide aff tae the game wae thur tickets. Ya beauty. It's a dream come true. (*looking up, hands clasped*) Thank you God. Wan mer miracle an ah'm gonnae believe in you.
Phil	(*to Terry*) Clamp. (*to Cathy*) Wur yez on the town last night, then?
Cathy	Naw. We had jet lag efter wur flight.
Theresa	She had jet lag. Ah had tae babysit. Up aw night wae her, so ah wiz.
Terry	(*to Phil*) Ah wish it wiz me.
Phil	(*to Terry*) Shoosh! (*to Cathy*) Hiv yez goat plans fur the night?
Theresa	Aye, but they don't include you.
Cathy	Come on, Theresa. The guys are jist tryin tae be friendly.
Terry	That's right, hen. You tell her.
Theresa	(*to Cathy*) Come on, let's get back tae the pool.
Terry	(*to Phil*) Did ye hear that, Phil? Can ye see that big darlin in a wee swimmin cozzy?

Phil	(*to Terry*) Naw, but ah can see you oan a stretcher. (*to Cathy*) Listen, ah don't mean tae be forward, ur that, but as ye can see, we're roughin it a bit, an we'd be dead grateful if we could mibbe go tae yer hotel wae yez fur a wee wash an a bite tae eat. We'll buy yez a drink an that.
Terry	(*to Phil*) Good yin. Yer coastin, ma man. Ah'm proud ae ye.
Theresa	Ah'll see ye when yer better dressed.
Cathy	Uch. Look at the state ae them, Theresa.
Theresa	Exactly. Ah want tae take they big bath towels hame as a souvenir, Cathy. Ah'm no hivin Dirty Dan wipin his arse wae wan.
Phil	We'll bring wur ain towels.
Terry	(*to Phil*) We've no goat any towels.
Phil	(*to Terry*) Button it.
Theresa	It's trowels, no towels, yous'll need tae get the dirt aff. Yous are absolutely boufin. Ah see yer pal there can play in any position. He's got a number eleven oan his tap lip and a number two in his troosers. And he's dribblin doon his chin.
Terry	(*to Phil*) She's game, Phil. She's game.
Phil	(*to Terry*) She's too game for you. (*to Cathy*) Look, we're jist a couple a Celtic

	supporters like yerselves, far fae hame, an lookin fur a wee bit a camaraderie.
Theresa	Ah can imagine the kinda camaraderie yer pal's goat in mind. His tongue's hingin oot there.
Phil	He's jist thirsty. We both ur – we need fed an wattered.
Terry	(*To Phil*) Down boy.
Phil	(*To Terry*) If you spoil this fur me, ah'm gonnae smother ye in yer sleep. (*To Cathy*) Look, wur aw here fur the same reason. Tae see the Celtic. Noo ah know we look like a couple a Jack Palancers, but we're brand new. Gen up.
Cathy	(*to Theresa*) Come on, Theresa. Gie the guys a brek. We're aw oan the same side.
Theresa	Tell ye whit. We'll be in a wee bar doon at the main squerr called El Slingo's. We'll catch yez there the back a six.
Terry	(*to Phil*) Eureka!
Phil	(*to Terry*) You reek a somethin. (*to Cathy*) See ye at six then.
Cathy	Aye. See yez later.
Theresa	Bye-bye, boys. (*She walks off swinging her hips, with Cathy following behind, looking back at Phil, and waving*).

[*Cathy and Theresa exit*]

Phil	You were right out of order, there.
Terry	Whit dae ye mean? Ah never opened ma mooth.
Phil	Aye ye did. Yer bottom lip wiz like a doorstep, an yer tongue wiz like a paintbrush.
Terry	Nae wunner. Did ye see the chassis oan that big doll? Thurz a few miles oan the clock there, Phil. Has she goat a license fur that wiggle?
Phil	Ah don't think she's gonnae gie you the green light.
Terry	She wiz playin hard tae get, Phil. Ah know women. Some ae ma best friends are women. Treat them mean, keep them keen. That's their philosophy. We're well in there. Quoted. Ah'm tellin ye. We've goat it made.
Phil	Ah'm no so sure. Ah think Cathy's taen a wee fancy tae me, but ah don't think Theresa's wearin you, Terry. Ah sensed a wee bit a friction there.
Terry	She'll be wearin me the night, Phil. An there'll be mer than a wee bit a friction between us, ah can tell ye. We'll be generatin enough electricity tae floodlight Parkheid fur a whole season.
Phil	Jist watch ye don't get yer fingers burned. Ah don't want ye crampin ma style.

Terry	Nae danger, Phil. Ah can hardly wait tae six a cloack. A wee warm-up in yon taverna. Couple a haufs. Wee bit a patter. Wance we hit that hotel, we go oor separate ways. If that wee yin's no intae ye, ah'll meet ye back at the tent the morra mornin. That's whit friends are fur.
Phil	Wae a friend like you, who needs enemies? But see if you screw things up fur me an that wee Cathy, ah'll rattle your beads.

[Lights out]

' Leòmhainn Lisbon:
Gemmell, Simpson,
Lennox, Jinky agus càch,

b' iad na gillean
a cheannsaich *Inter*
ann an naoi deug trì fichead is a seachd.

Ann an lèine nan cearcall
a leithid nach fhacas
o chluich Setanta aig Ceann na Pàirc,

gach ainm cliùiteach
cluinnte nar n-ùrnaigh
seach Màta, Lùcas, Eòin no Marc.

Na Ceiltich ghlòrmhor
laoich na h-Eòrpa
– cha chuir sinn stoc anns a' phòca gu bràth! '

NIALL O'GALLAGHER
POET

> The Lisbon Lions: Gemmell, Simpson, Chalmers, Johnstone and the rest, they are the bhoys who conquered Inter in 1967. No one had seen their like in the hoops since Cuchulainn himself had played at Parkhead, each famous name now heard in our prayers, in place of Matthew, Mark, Luke and John. The glorious Celtic, the champions of Europe, we'll never put our scarves in our pockets again!

NIALL O'GALLAGHER
POET

●

> In 1967, I left school, uncaring of Celtic's grand victory over Inter Milan. I discovered Don Giovanni, Mozart's opera and Baudelaire at university; a secret love two years later. The hymn of re-awakening in Beethoven's 6th Symphony rising, growing to fill a still, wide sky is glorious. The last movement of Symphony number 7 is wild. I want to always be wild. I am now 67.

ANNE PIA
POET AND MUSICIAN

' It might sound strange coming from a lifelong Hoops fan, but I didn't really have strong feelings about Lisbon until I watched it on video in the late '80s. I knew all about it but until I could see it the emotions stayed in check. So thanks to VHS, I got to get a real sense of the passion of it and that'll stay with me forever. '

PAUL POWER
PICTURE FRAMER

' Unalloyed joy! A sense that things could get better. From Lisbon a beautiful, penetrating ray of sunlight shone on Belfast, then a cold, dark place where Catholics like my family suffered discrimination, lacked political and economic equality, were told to keep down and know our place. We are more than a football team. Solidarity, friendship, universalism, Brother Walfrid, Lisbon Lions, Celtic, you are a beacon of hope. '

KEVIN ROONEY
WRITER AND TEACHER

14

Picking Sides

[Father O'Hara and Danny in the taverna, worse the wear for drink]

Danny My but it's busy here, Father.

Father O'Hara I wonder how much that waiter makes?

Danny He'll do alright this week, wi all the football fans an that. Why do you ask, Father?

Father O'Hara Oh, jist curious. Ye know, Daniel. It's no easy being a priest. It's an eight-day week. Ah work Christmas an Easter. An right through the Glasgow Fair. There's yer holiday of obligation, of course. But that's no so much a holiday as an obligation. Where dae ye think that waiter's gone? Ah mind the time when the flash of a cassock wid hiv goat ye served like that. (*Clicks his fingers*) Aye,

	being a priest isnae as glamorous as it's made out tae be, ye know. It's no aw wine … an roses.
Danny	I never really thought of it that way, Father.
Father O'Hara	Whit dae ye dae fur a living yersel, Daniel?
Danny	Ah work in a clothes factory.
Father O'Hara	Dae ye noo? That's interesting.
Danny	It's pretty boring actually. Repetitive, like.
Father O'Hara	Don't talk tae me aboot repetitive. Ah'm like a stuck record. Whit's yer tap line, Daniel?
Danny	With overtime, about eight pounds Irish.
Father O'Hara	Dae ye know whit ah come oot wae?
Danny	No. What?

[*Father O'Hara whispers in Danny's ear*]

Danny	Is that gross?
Father O'Hara	Gross? It's diabolical.

[*Enter Donaldo*]

Father O'Hara	Here's one of the other side.
Donaldo	Hello, Father.
Father O'Hara	Yer Scottish.
Donaldo	And Italian. Donaldo Gaberdini. Howzitgaun?

Father O'Hara	Yer backing a loser, son. Yer ontae plums. The Tic are gonnae lift this cup.
Donaldo	Inter are invincible.
Danny	Celtic are an Irish club. They've got the luck of the Irish, and the rub of the green.
Father O'Hara	Celtic are a Catholic club. They've got faithful supporters and a place booked in paradise.
Donaldo	Inter Milan are a football club. I've come to watch them play. I've come to watch them win.
Father O'Hara	Do you really think you stand a chance?
Donaldo	Is the Pope Italian?
Danny	We've got Saint Patrick on our side, Mister.
Donaldo	Zat right? We've got Mazzola. The cup's goin back tae Milan.
Father O'Hara	Ah'll believe that when Rangers sign a Catholic.

[*Farquhar appears*]

Farquhar	Did somebody mention the Teddy Bears?
Father O'Hara	Get away with ye!
Farquhar	I didn't come all the way from Larkhall to Lisbon to be dictated to by a priest. Especially one who's been worshipping the Holy Spirit. I saw you turning wine into water half a mile down the road. In a public place.

Donaldo	Geez peace.
Farquhar	(*To Donaldo*) And where did you pick up that Scottish accent, might I ask?
Donaldo	In Scotland, where ah was born and bred.
Farquhar	You mean to say you're British?
Donaldo	I mean tae say I'm an Italian Scot. My faither fled fae Mussolini.
Farquhar	And found sanctuary in Britain.
Donaldo	Naw, no sanctuary. Sectarianism. Bigotry. Prejudice. Intolerance. Broken windows. Paint daubed on his door. Insults in the street.
Father O'Hara	There's another community wae a similar experience of the warmth of British society. They talk about sanctuary, but they welcome you with open sewers. Stuff ye intae ghettoes. They promise ye green fields an gie ye the Gorbals.
Danny	(*Scratching his head, half-mocking*) Now who could that be?
Farquhar	Nobody asked you to come. If you don't like it, leave it.
Donaldo	Leave my home? That'll be right.
Farquhar	Then be British.
Donaldo	Like you? I'm happy with my two nations. Are you happy with being British? Whose side were you on a fortnight ago when Scotland beat England?

Farquhar	Scotland's, of course.
Father O'Hara	Then be Scottish. Mine's a whisky.
Farquhar	I'd rather drink with the Devil himself. Yous had better behave yourselves at the game, or I'll be down on you like...
Father O'Hara	... A Rangers full-back?

[*Farquhar goes back to his table*]

Donaldo	(*To Danny and Father O'Hara*) I'll get myself a refill. It's been nice talking to you. Pity one side has to lose. There's no neutrality in football. May the best team win.

[*Donaldo goes to the bar*]

Father O'Hara	That was nice ae the lad, wasn't it? Wishing victory on Celtic like that.
Danny	There's nothing like a good loser, Father. And that big polis was nothing like a good loser.
Father O'Hara	Nothing at all. Now, all this talking has given me a helluva thirst, Daniel. Whit's keepin that waiter, apart fae a decent wage? That's a smart jacket yer wearin. A clothes factory, did ye say? Ah must give ye ma measurements before ye go.

[Lights out]

' In 1967 I was a wee boy living in Barrowfield a stone's throw away from Parkhead. It was a proud moment for my Dad to see me on stage at the end of the Pavilion run with that very team he had watched winning the cup. When I think about it Terry wasn't that far away from myself – 'can I watch yer motor mister?'. A wee chancer. '

DOUGLAS SANNACHAN
ACTOR

' Stories passed down by our fathers and grandfathers of homegrown heroes who conquered Europe were told with such vividness that it became almost possible to imagine ourselves bearing witness to Celtic's greatest ever triumph. Lisbon is a victory that transcends generations, and, although born twenty some years later, to be in the presence of these men, their playing days behind them, is to behold gods among mortals. '

PAUL SHERIDAN
MUSICIAN (THE WAKES)

'In recent years in football there has been a certain race for the stars. Aberdeen have two stars on their strip, which I think signifies a European Cup Winners Cup win and Super Cup win. Rangers have five stars on their shirt: something to do with (though I'm not sure) decades and league titles won. Celtic wear one star. It says simply: 'In Scotland, we are peerless'.'

GRAHAM SPIERS
JOURNALIST

'Celtic – the first Scottish, British and Northern European club to win the European Cup. A team that hailed from both the Irish and Scottish, Catholic and Protestant traditions of the people it represented on the park. The Lions demonstrably articulate the universal truth; we achieve more when we unite in work and play together against the tendency to divide and discriminate.
The Lisbon Lions – you are immortal.'

DAVID STEEL
FAN

' When anybody asks me what age I was
when Celtic lifted the European Cup in Lisbon
I am able to reply without even a blink:
'I was seven years, two weeks and four days
old!' So I do remember it, the deserted Possil
streets one minute and not a spare piece of
tarmac the next. What does '67 mean to me
– I still cry 50 years later. '

JOE SULLIVAN
CELTIC VIEW DEPUTY EDITOR

' I wasn't yet four, didn't have a clue, but could
taste the magic in the air. Streets deserted,
everyone indoors. Our coin-operated telly, sixpenny
pieces piled high. Told to keep quiet, then screams,
laughter, hugs. Years later Billy McNeill would give
my wee mum a lift to work in Pollokshields. 'He's
just an ordinary bloke' she'd say, knowing full well
he was a Lion of a man. '

THERESA TALBOT
WRITER AND BROADCASTER

15

Demand a Milanda

[*Cathy and Theresa are arguing as they enter the taverna. Donaldo is at the bar*]

Cathy
That wiz dead mean, Theresa. They boys were jist bein friendly.

Theresa
Too friendly.

Cathy
Ah cannae believe you lied like that.

Theresa
El Slingo? Ah thoat you spoke the lingo. You shoulda tippled right away.

Cathy
Ah thoat ye wur bein straight wae the guys.

Theresa
Ah wiz gettin shot ae the guys, Cathy. Ah can spot chancers like that a mile aff. Bongo and Pongo. Couple a gold-diggers. Fancied their chances. Especially

	that big yin. He'd get his money back oan the Ghost Train.
Cathy	Phil was awright. He had nice eyes.
Theresa	Pity they wur trapped in that boady. Did ye see his legs? We coulda taen wan each an made a wish. Anyhow. The wan ye wur leavin me wae wiz a pure creep. Foghorn Leghorn. Ah needed a bath efter hivin his eyes crawlin aw ower me.
Cathy	Mibbe we'll bump intae them again.
Theresa	Knowin oor luck we'll be staunin next tae them at the game.
Cathy	Dae ye really think so?
Theresa	Ah hope no. Ur they'll be gettin a rubber ear tae go wae that dizzy we gied them. (*Spotting Donaldo*) Haud oan. Pinch me, Cathy. Am ah still awake?
Cathy	Aye, but ye've went aw thon way.
Theresa	Is he gorgeous ur is he gorgeous? An Adonis in the flesh.
Cathy	He's no in the flesh. He's wearin an Inter Milan tap. He's a Tally. Yer no gonnae faw fur a Tally. We're here tae support Celtic.
Theresa	You and whose army, hen? (*To Donaldo*) Hey gorgeous! Parliamo Glasgow?
Donaldo	Sorry?
Theresa	Dae ye speak English?

Donaldo	(*under his breath*) Aw naw. Here we go again. (*to Theresa, his hands a foot apart*) A bit.
Theresa	Say no more. (*To Cathy*) Look at they legs. Ah bet they go aw the way up tae his arse. Ah'll be gled tae see the back ae him. Ah'll catch ye later oan at the hotel.
Cathy	Theresa Kelly. You are not on. We've stood up two perfectly nice guys fae Glasgow. Celtic supporters. An noo you're gonnae waltz aff wae an Inter Milan fan, an leave me oan ma ain? Not on your Nelly, Kelly… Some pal you ur. A tan, a flashy smile, an yer dead tae the world. Talk tae me right now, Theresa, an stoap makin eyes at that guy. He's wan a them.
Theresa	(*to Donaldo*) Whit part ae Italy are you fae?
Donaldo	Largs.
Theresa	Largs?
Donaldo	Aye. Largs. Ye know, the place where Celtic train.
Cathy	Largs isnae in Italy.
Donaldo	Did I say I was from Italy?
Theresa	You're Scottish?
Donaldo	And Italian. I've got the best of both worlds.
Cathy	That's jist pure greed, wantin it baith ways. Come on, Theresa. Ye cannae hiv a

holiday romance wae somedy fae Largs.
He'll be pesterin ye when ye get hame.

Theresa   He can pester me here tae his heart's
content.

Donaldo   Look. I don't want to split yous up. Could
ah buy you two girls a drink?

Theresa   Ma pal's goat an appointment in El
Slingo's, haven't ye, Cathy?

Cathy   Naw, it's been cancelled. Ah'd love a
drink. A glass a gooseberry wine wid go
doon a treat.

[*Donaldo orders drinks*]

Theresa   Is that no Father O'Hara ower there?

Cathy   Aye, Theresa. An is that no an angel
sittin beside him?

Theresa   Ah've never seen your face light up like
that, Cathy Boyle. Ah think you better
hiv a seat an a drink tae steady yer
nerves. We baith need wan.

Father O'Hara   Cathy! Come and join us.

Danny   My, but that girl is the dead spit of me
mother.

[*Terry and Phil walk in*]

Terry   Am ah seein things? Ma back's like a
pin-cushion. We've been sold a dummy,
Phil. They've moved the goalposts. We've
been caught in an offside trap. The dirty
rotten snide backstabbing…

Phil	Cool it, Terry. It's Ladies' Choice, an we're the losers. Anyhow, bae the looks ae things he's wan a yous, if ye know whit ah mean.
Terry	Don't start me...
Phil	Ah said cool it. Let's jist hope the Celtic win.
Terry	The way oor luck's goin, ah don't fancy thur chances.
Danny	Come an join us, lads. Hiv yez any of that marvellous macaroon on yez? Or that lovely spearmint?
Phil	We gave it away tae they wee urchins at the squerr.
Terry	Aye, they taught us a wee bit a Portugese.
Phil and Terry	Portugeeza dod a this, an Portugeeza dod a that.
Terry	We were cleaned oot in five minutes flat.
Phil	Left wae an empty barra an a clear conscience.
Father	That wiz awfy good ae yez. Cleaned oot aw thegither, were yez? Nothing left at aw? Charity begins at home, ye know. Ah can think ae a poor parish priest that wid've been glad ae some sustenance. Aye, it's a priest's life. That waiter's away tae the Algarve, ah think. Ah'll go up an order some drinks. Wid you give me a hand, Daniel?

Danny	Sure Father. (*Getting up*) Have ye enough money there?
Terry	(*Looking at Donaldo in disbelief*) Haud oan. You're a Celtic supporter?
Donaldo	No this week. Inter is ma furst love. It wiz ma da's team. Ah'm a Celtic supporter tae it comes tae Europe.
Terry	Your heid must be full a wee motors.
Phil	It could be worse. He could be a Milan man and a Rangers Man.
Terry	He could be Dan-Dan, the funny wee man.
Phil	How many ae you Scots-Italians hiv come ower fur the game?
Donaldo	Must be a few hundred. (*To Theresa*) See ye in here after the gemme, okay?

[*Donaldo exits*]

Father O'Hara	A few hundred, eh? Hauf the cafes in Glesca must be shut.
Terry	(*to Phil, horrified*) Spinetti!
Phil	Naw, Terry. It's awright. Big Tony's a Juventus supporter. He telt me he wanted the Celts tae win.
Terry	(*to Theresa*) Ye couldnae lend us a pair a nylons, could ye? Nae questions asked.
Theresa	Naw, but ah've got a bra that might fit ye.
Cathy	Theresa!

Terry	(*Rubbing his hands*) Ah cannae wait fur the gemme.
Phil	If we get tickets.
Terry	We'll get in, don't you worry. Ah didnae come aw this way tae staun ootside.
Phil	We'll need tae get by big Farquhar furst. The mason in the black.
Terry	He's a dumpling. Ah'll tear him apart an spend the sixpence if ah hiv tae. Cannae wait tae kick-aff. Lennox'll be like a dug oot ae trap six at Shawfield.
Phil	They'll take some beating, though, that mob. Yon Hererra tae, he's a master tactician.
Father O'Hara	(*Hands clasped, looking up*) The cross. The cross.
Theresa	Whit is it Faither?
Father O'Hara	The cross.
Terry	Is he awright?
Phil	Ah think he's hivin a vision.
Terry	It's a wunner he can see at aw efter whit he pit away.
Father O'Hara	The cross. The fierce header. McPhail.
Terry	McPhail's no playin. Yon priest's got a bead loose.
Phil	Naw. He's right. It can be done. We've done it in the past. Think a Patsy Gallacher. Ma da says he could turn oan

a tanner. Then there wiz Jimmy McGrory, and whit aboot the great Charlie Tully? If ye know the history...

Terry   It's enough tae make yer heart go. Oh, oh, oh. Ah've found ma faith.

Phil   Ye've loast yer heid.

Terry   Ah've seen the light.

Phil   Ye've had too much ae the sun.

Terry   He descended like an angel. He came doon tae live amongst men. He suffered fur us. He performed miracles fur us. That's why we must sing his praise.

Phil   Who?

Terry   Jimmy, oh Jimmy Johnstone, oh Jimmy Johnstone on the wing.

Father O'Hara   Come on now. Order. If we're gonnae hiv a singsong let's dae it right. What about you, Daniel? What about a song from the Old Country?

Danny   Alright.

[*He sings 'Danny Boy'. During the song, Cathy moves closer and closer. He finishes. Applause*]

Danny   Any more for any more?

[*At this point another person, possibly Theresa, sings another song, Irish, pop or football. When it finishes, there is applause, then a spotlight on Cathy and Danny, who are talking about the game, but what game? During this exchange the couple become progressively more intimate*]

137

Cathy	Oh Danny, see when wee Jimmy's on the ball, twisting an turning, pure poetry in motion.
Danny	Aye, Cathy. An when Big Billy rises tae the occasion, he's head and shoulders above the rest.
Cathy	Whit a feeling.
Danny	A game of two halves.
Cathy	A clash of titans.
Danny	Time stands still.
Cathy	The atmosphere.
Danny	The feeling.
Cathy	The emotion.
Danny	The passion.
Cathy	The excitement.
Danny	Whit a team.
Cathy	Pure magic.
Danny	The slow build-up.
Cathy	A wee wan-two.
Danny	Chesting it down.
Cathy	A swerve ae the hips.
Danny	A tightening ae the thighs.
Cathy	Teasing the opposition.
Danny	Stretching the backs.
Cathy	An inch-perfect pass.

Danny	Peeling off two defenders.
Cathy	Ducking and diving.
Danny	A glimpse of paradise.
Cathy	A taste of honey.
Danny	One-touch football.
Cathy	Using both flanks.
Danny	Cutting inside the defence.
Cathy	That new boy. They say his first touch is brilliant.
Danny	Do they now?
Cathy	Close control.
Danny	A fine pair of legs.
Cathy	Comfortable on the ball.
Danny	And yer man the goalie.
Cathy	Doesn't let anything by him.
Danny	Safe hands.
Cathy	That big centre.
Danny	Cool as a cucumber.
Cathy	He's good at going forward.
Danny	Is that a fact? And what about the defence?
Cathy	It's at sixes and sevens.
Danny	The keeper's off his line.
Cathy	The defence is out of its depth.
Danny	He runs into space.

Cathy	Man on! Man on!
Danny	The crowd are going crazy.
Cathy	They're delirious.
Danny	There's a goalmouth scramble. Is that a red card?
Cathy	Naw. It's a green light.
Danny	He looks like scoring.
Cathy	There's an angel on the wing.
Danny	He takes aim.
Cathy	He shoots.
Danny	An arrow.
Cathy	She closes her eyes.
Danny	It's there.

[*They kiss*]

Father O'Hara	Come on you lot. We're gonnae miss the gemme.
Phil and Terry	Oh Danny Boy, the Celts, the Celts, are calling.

[*Cathy takes Danny's ticket and gives it, together with her own, to Terry and Phil*]

Terry	Ya beauty!
Phil	Ya dancer!

[*Terry and Phil pocket the tickets and exit. Cathy grabs Danny and drags him off. Theresa shouts after her*]

Theresa   Cathy Boyle, ah'm gonnae shop you tae
            Father O'Hara. Ah mean it.

[She exits. Lights out]

I was eight days old when Celtic won, it passed me by, however the feat will reverberate forever. It is highly unlikely that any club in the world will equal what Jock Stein and The Lisbon Lions accomplished, not just in sport, but also regarding class and identity. 'We want to do it playing good football, to make neutrals glad we won it.' Jock Stein, May '67.

KEITH WARWICK
ACTOR

As a Hun, I didn't care for Celtic with their green and their old Jock Stein, didn't care much about backstreet Scots humbling Italian artisans. Scots that didn't need an equaliser to give them new heart as, apparently, the old heart was beating loud and strong. Didn't even know the swarthy Italians were shamed by Scots who had to replace their falsers for the winning team photo.

BRIAN WHITTINGHAM
WRITER

' So the boyfriend, wannabe professional sports photographer and cartoonist, holidays all used up, chucked the day job and sallied off to Lisbon with his cameras. He came home and plied me with Mateus Rose – the first table wine this Bathgate boy had encountered. And served it the next time I dined at his place. And the next. An unpromising gambit you might suppose. Reader, I married him! '

RUTH WISHART
JOURNALIST

16

A Wing and a Prayer

[Keith Chinwag introduces radio commentary]

Keith Chinwag   Good afternoon and welcome to the
Estádio Nacional here in Lisbon for the
final of the European Cup. My name is
Keith Chinwag, and I'll be giving you live
commentary for the BBC World Service
on this wonderful occasion. It's a great
day for British football, with Glasgow
Celtic up against the Italian Champions
Inter Milan. It's a marvellous day, with
the sun beating down on the 45,000
supporters packed into this beautiful
stadium, built in honour of President
Salazar, the Fascist dictator. We
remember of course that Italy was on the
side of Fascism in the last war, and if the
result from that confrontation is
repeated today then Celtic fans can

prepare themselves for a victory parade... Now the teams. First Inter Milan, in their third final in the twelve years of this competition. Sarti, Burgnich, and Facchetti, Bedin, Guarneri, and Picchi, Domenghini, Bicicli, Mazzola, Cappellini, and Corso. Now the Celtic line-up. (*A cheer greets each name*) Simpson, Craig, and Gemmell, Murdoch, McNeill, and Clark, Johnstone, Wallace, Chalmers, Auld, and Lennox... Penalty for Inter Milan. Eight minutes gone. A crushing blow... And it's a disaster for Celtic, and for Scotland. Jim Craig bringing down Cappellini. A Jack Charlton or a Bobby Moore would have reacted quicker and calmer there. Mazzola with the penalty. It's 1–0 Inter Milan. And Gordon Banks might well have stopped that... Half-time. The Inter defence is under pressure, but looks impenetrable... And the second half gets underway, with the Scots looking decidedly dodgy. One wonders how an English club would cope with Inter, even a Second Division one. Admirably, one suspects... Murdoch to Craig. Gemmell. Oh my word. Celtic have equalised. 62 minutes gone, and I think they're going to have to ask for a new ball. That one just about burst the net. 1–1 ... And the Brits are back in business. Gemmell is a bit ungainly. He might not have the finesse of a Geoff Hurst, but he hit that with a lot of heart… Five minutes remaining. Murdoch. Tries a shot. Chalmers. It's there. Celtic take the lead… And it looks as though the European Cup is going to Britain for the first time.

[Lights out]

'It wasn't ever mentioned in my house, or by my grandparents, or at school. I was only in Primary One, so carried on oblivious; even when it was mentioned by a pal from my street that went to a 'different' school I had no idea what he was talking about. We had to wait a few years, and for Barcelona, before talk of European trophies was permitted. '

STEPHEN WRIGHT
MUSICIAN

17

The Best Team in the Land

Paradise, 1992

[*Danny and Sean at the match*]

Sean	Imagine missing the game of the century because of a woman.
Danny	Don't call your mother a woman.
Sean	Could you both no have waited?
Danny	Time waits for no man, boy.
Sean	You should have been there, da.
Danny	You wouldn't be here if I'd been there.
Sean	What do you mean.
Danny	Think about it, son.
Sean	Do you mean…? Are you sayin…? Did I…?
Danny	You sprang from the loins of Lisbon, Sean. Ye were a souvenir, if ye like. Yer maw got

you smuggled through Customs no bother at all. You were a wee leprechaun we didn't know about at the time. We named you after another Irishman, Sean Fallon. That was our way of remembering. We came home with each other, our memories, and you.

Sean   I cannae believe it. I'm the reason you missed Celtic's greatest moment? Tae think that you lost out on the European Cup Final ower the heid a me.

Danny   I didn't lose anything. I won and so did Celtic, and them bookies lost a bloody fortune.

Sean   You missed the game, da. Ye could've been there and ye wurnae there!

Danny   I was there or thereabouts. There's some things in life more important than football, Sean. Life's a cup. Ye lift it to your lips when ye can.

Sean   Wait'll I see ma maw.

Danny   Don't you dare say a word. She made me promise not to tell.

Sean   I bet she did. I'll tell the whole world.

Danny   About that motor.

Sean   Jesus, would you stoop to bribery?

Danny   I can stoop as well as any man. By Christ, you've yer mother's eyes. Aye, an yer da's money.

Sean   A winning combination.

Danny   I'll be wanting a run to all the matches, mind. I've worked me arse off and I've nothing to chauffeur it.

Sean   Da, ah promise ye, ye'll never miss another game...

Danny   It's a deal. Here's the teams. Come on the Hoops!

[*The tannoy plays 'Sure it's a Grand Old Team'. The music slows. A green light comes on.*]

Danny   Hey, that's not Paul McStay. It's Willie Wallace! And there's Jimmy Johnstone!

[*Sean steps aside as Cathy comes on, followed by the rest of the cast. They sing 'We've got the best team in the land' to the tune of 'He's got the whole world in his hands', from Ronnie Simpson through to Bobby Lennox. While the song is in progress, the Chorus steps forward*]

Chorus   It was a day to remember. The day we went to Lisbon. Those who couldn't be there in body, were there in spirit. They came pouring out of factory gates, out of the docks and the shipyards, up from the pits, out of offices and shops. Crowds huddled round radios and TV sets. For two hours on that famous afternoon, Glasgow belonged to Celtic. There was one word on everyone's lips. Celtic! Those who couldn't go on a wing, went on a prayer. They prayed for the jersey. They had nothing to fear. With Ronnie Simpson, they were in safe hands. In Jim Craig, they

had a one-man Ministry of Defence.
Tommy Gemmell had his right foot
registered as a lethal weapon. Bobby
Murdoch could stop a tank in its tracks,
which came in handy when you were up
against the Rangers. Billy McNeill was a
tower of strength. When Cesar was at
centre-half, he came, he saw, he
conquered. John Clark was made to
measure in midfield. Jimmy Johnstone
was a genius on the wing. Willie Wallace
was a monument in his own right. Steve
Chalmers made many a goalie greet as
they picked the baw oot the onion bag.
There was only one 'T' in Scotland,
Ber'T'ie Auld, and with him on the boil,
the game was in the bag. Bobby Lennox
should have been booked for speeding,
because the buzzbomb with the short
fuse had the fastest legs in football. The
man in charge of Kelly's Kids was Jock
Stein, a miner's son. With Scottish steel
forged in Irish fire, the Stein Machine was
unstoppable. The fans knew they were
onto a winner. The Bhoys did them proud.
They went out as underdogs, and came
back as kings of the jungle. The best club
in the country showed that there was only
one team in Europe. Celtic whipped the
cream of the continent. Their names have
become a litany, a prayer about Celtic's
past. Their fame lives on. If you know the
history, then you know the story of *The
Lions of Lisbon*, the pride of Parkhead.

Full Time

67 on '67 Contributors

DAVE ANDERSON ACTOR, PLAYWRIGHT, JAZZ MUSICIAN

EILEEN AULD SUPPORTER

DOUGLAS BEATTIE JOURNALIST

ALAN BISSETT WRITER

JOSEPH M. BRADLEY ACADEMIC

STEPHEN BREEN MANAGING DIRECTOR

EDDIE BURNS TEACHER

JOHN CAIRNEY ACTOR

AONGHAS PHÀDRAIG CAIMBEUL / ANGUS PETER
CAMPBELL WRITER

ROISÍN COLL ACADEMIC

HARRY CONNOLLY BUCHANAN BRIDGE CLUB

DONALD COWEY JOURNALIST

PAUL CUDDIHY EDITOR *CELTIC VIEW*

TONY CURRAN ACTOR

MARTIN DALZIEL REPORTER, *CELTIC VIEW*

BOB DAVIS ACADEMIC

SIR TOM DEVINE HISTORIAN

PHILIP DIFFER WRITER

DES DILLON WRITER

CHRIS DOLAN WRITER

AIDAN DONALDSON WRITER

MARY EDWARD WRITER

PAUL ENGLISH JOURNALIST

JIM FERGUSON POET

ALISTAIR FINDLAY WRITER

JEANETTE FINDLAY ACADEMIC

RODDY FORSYTH JOURNALIST

JANICE GALLOWAY WRITER

JOHN GILLEN TRADE UNION ACTIVIST

RODGE GLASS WRITER

TONY HAMILTON CEO OF CELTIC FC FOUNDATION

PATRICK HARKINS FILMMAKER

CHRIS HART SENIOR LECTURER IN MENTAL HEALTH

BILL HEANEY WRITER

AARON HEPBURN FAN

ALISON IRVINE WRITER

LINDA JACKSON SINGER

ANDREW JAMIESON SUPPORTER

PAT KANE WRITER

AARON KELLY ACADEMIC

TOM LEONARD POET

JIM LISTER THEATRE PRODUCER

HUGH MACDONALD JOURNALIST

LIBBY McARTHUR ACTOR, WRITER, DIRECTOR

MARGOT McCUAIG CHILD OF LISBON, FILMMAKER

MARTIN McCARDIE ACTOR, WRITER, DIRECTOR

BRIAN McGEACHAN WRITER

KEVIN McKENNA JOURNALIST

HENRY McLEISH FORMER FIRST MINISTER OF SCOTLAND

WILLY MALEY ACADEMIC

IAIN MALONEY WRITER

LAURA MARNEY WRITER

SANDY MOFFAT ARTIST

CRAIG MUNRO ACTOR

DES MURPHY FORMER TEACHER

MICHAEL NARDONE ACTOR

GED O'BRIEN TEACHER

NIALL O'GALLAGHER POET

ANNE PIA POET AND MUSICIAN

PAUL POWER PICTURE FRAMER

KEVIN ROONEY WRITER AND TEACHER

DOUGLAS SANNACHAN ACTOR

PAUL SHERIDAN MUSICIAN (THE WAKES)

GRAHAM SPIERS JOURNALIST

DAVID STEEL PROGRAMME DIRECTOR

JOE SULLIVAN *CELTIC VIEW* DEPUTY EDITOR

THERESA TALBOT WRITER, BROADCASTER

KEITH WARWICK ACTOR

BRIAN WHITTINGHAM WRITER

RUTH WISHART JOURNALIST

STEPHEN WRIGHT MUSICIAN, THEATRE PRODUCER

Some other books published by **LUATH** PRESS

Playing for the Hoops: The George McCluskey story

Aidan Donaldson
ISBN: 978-1-910745-63-2 HBK £16.99

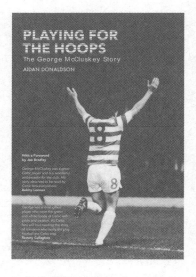

How did George McCluskey become a true Celtic legend? What binds the fans and players and creates this strong sense of belonging? And what does the Irish diaspora have to do with the club?

George McCluskey ranks alongside Kenny Dalglish, Tommy Burns, Johnny Doyle and Paul McStay in a generation of Celtic greats. Aidan Donaldson's biography is the first definitive account of McCluskey's hugely successful professional career over two decades as a striker.

Playing in the Hoops for eight years, George scored 54 goals in this time. He also changed the entire game in favour of Celtic over and over again. Later going on to play for Hibernian – as well as Leeds, Hamilton, Kilmarnock and Clyde – he was the injured party in one of the most scandalous tackles in football history.

A truly Celtic minded man and player, George McCluskey embodies the Celtic spirit.

In football biographies the reader often only sees the player and not the real person. I was extremely fortunate to play football for the club I supported my entire life... Coming from a Celtic-minded family and community it has been an absolute privilege to have played for Celtic on so many occasions and to have shared in their joy, hopes and dreams – as well as in their disappointments.

FROM THE INTRODUCTION BY
GEORGE McCLUSKEY

Singin I'm No a Billy He's a Tim

Des Dillon
ISBN: 9781908373052 PBK £7.99

What happens when a Rangers fan and Celtic fan are locked in a prison cell together on the day of an Old Firm Match? It is through Billy and Tim that Des Dillon explores sectarianism, bigotry, how it becomes part of one's identity and is inculcated by family and society. However, the book is not limited to Scotland but refers to every peace process in the world, where common ground and a shared humanity is found through responding to the needs of others. Now it is up to these two fans to start their personal peace process to find some common ground to slowly let go of their bigotry.

His raucous sense of humour and keen understanding of the west-coast sectarian mindset make his message seem a matter of urgency and not just a liberal platitude.
THE GUARDIAN

The potency of Dillon's writing beats louder than any drum that the bigots can bang.
IRISH POST

Explosive.
EVENING NEWS

Details of these and other books published by Luath Press can be found at: **www.luath.co.uk**

Luath Press Limited
committed to publishing well written books worth reading

LUATH PRESS takes its name from Robert Burns, whose little collie Luath (*Gael.*, swift or nimble) tripped up Jean Armour at a wedding and gave him the chance to speak to the woman who was to be his wife and the abiding love of his life. Burns called one of 'The Twa Dogs' Luath after Cuchullin's hunting dog in Ossian's *Fingal*. Luath Press was established in 1981 in the heart of Burns country, and now resides a few steps up the road from Burns' first lodgings on Edinburgh's Royal Mile.

Luath offers you distinctive writing with a hint of unexpected pleasures.

Most bookshops in the UK, the US, Canada, Australia, New Zealand and parts of Europe either carry our books in stock or can order them for you. To order direct from us, please send a £sterling cheque, postal order, international money order or your credit card details (number, address of cardholder and expiry date) to us at the address below. Please add post and packing as follows: UK – £1.00 per delivery address; overseas surface mail – £2.50 per delivery address; overseas airmail – £3.50 for the first book to each delivery address, plus £1.00 for each additional book by airmail to the same address. If your order is a gift, we will happily enclose your card or message at no extra charge.

ILLUSTRATION: IAN KELLAS

Luath Press Limited
543/2 Castlehill
The Royal Mile
Edinburgh EH1 2ND
Scotland

Telephone: 0131 225 4326 (24 hours)
email: sales@luath.co.uk
Website: www.luath.co.uk